KRISTI ME

"Boylan tells the truth about both the pain and joy of the adolescent girl's coming of age. And she also provides us with a remarkable blueprint for honoring and nurturing a girl's spirit through the process, so that she stands a far better chance of growing into a strong and healthy woman."

—Christiane Northrup, M.D., author of *Women's Bodies,*
Women's Wisdom and *The Wisdom of Menopause*

"*The Seven Sacred Rites of Menopause* speaks directly to a woman's soul. It's a book that every woman who is either preparing to enter menopause, or is going through menopause, will want to read for guidance and illumination. Kristi Meisenbach Boylan has provided a menopausal roadmap for generations to come."

—Marianne Williamson, author of
A Return to Love and *Imagine*

"Kristi Meisenbach Boylan writes with an amazing degree of sensitivity and insight."   —Michael Gurian, author of *The Wonder of Girls;*
The Wonder of Boys; and *Boys and Girls Learn Differently*

"A unique book . . . fascinating."   —Sandra Cabot, M.D.,
author of *Smart Medicine for Menopause*

"Inspiring and uplifting."   —Bala Jaison, Ph.D., director of
Focusing for Creative Living

"In a conversational st--- the author explores the soul's journey in search of spiritual bala

Born to Be
Wild

**Freeing the Spirit of the
Hyperactive Child**

Kristi Meisenbach Boylan

A PERIGEE BOOK

7/03

P

A Perigee Book
Published by The Berkley Publishing Group
A division of Penguin Group (USA) Inc.
375 Hudson Street
New York, New York 10014

First edition: July 2003

Library of Congress Cataloging-in-Publication Data

Meisenbach Boylan, Kristi, 1960–
Born to be wild : freeing the spirit of the hyperactive child /
Kristi Meisenbach Boylan.—
1st ed.
p. cm
Includes bibliographical references and index.
ISBN 0-399-52891-1
1. Attention-deficit hyperactivity disorder. 2. Hyperactive children. I. Title.

RJ506.H9M45 2003
616.85'89—dc21 2003046016

Printed in the United States of America

10 9 8 7 6 5 4 3 2 1

For Brandan

"And now," cried Max,
"let the wild rumpus start."

Maurice Sendak
Where the Wild Things Are

Contents

Acknowledgments

LIBERATING BRANDAN'S SPIRIT was not the effort of one or two people. It was a unified achievement on the part of more friends, family, physicians, teachers, and neighbors than I could possibly name. However, there were a dozen or so saints who really went above and beyond the call of duty in assisting my husband and me in making sure that Brandan's spirit was free.

First and foremost, a special thanks to my agent, Jeff Herman, and editor, Sheila Curry Oakes, for understanding the importance of making sure the spirits of all children remain free.

I would also like to thank the teachers and educators at Miller Elementary School: Laurie Scaglion, Debbie Cook, Heather Reed, Susan Danzler, and most especially Sharon Swanson and Gwen Hooten. Even today as I write this, I am feeling overwhelmed by the way your love turned my son's life around. And truly if I ever do win the lottery, I will buy you all new cars.

Acknowledgments

Without the help of a very wise physician who miraculously plucked us out of the medical maze at a time when we were hopelessly lost, I doubt that Brandan would be where he is today. Dr. James Elderman, your guidance and wisdom will never be forgotten. And to Rex McCulley, thank you for giving me the tools to deal with the day-to-day ups and downs of living with a highly active child. Your support in the weeks after our crisis gave me added strength in a very difficult time.

There have also been many coaches who have been surrogate parents to Brandan over the years, most notably Rob Menditto and Ed Pecikonis. I am grateful to each and every one of you for healing Brandan's body as well as his spirit.

I am also grateful to my friend and mentor, Marianne Williamson, for her Christmas Eve miracle, and for reminding me that God would not have given me Brandan without also giving me the ability to heal him. Thank you also, Marianne, for reminding me that terminology really does make a difference in how a child sees himself.

To our neighbors, the Shatswells, the Cranks, the Malmroses, and the Pipers—I could list the reasons why, but then that would be a book unto itself—thank you, thank you, thank you. And to Katie Lady Padgett, for being there, even at 4 A.M.

I must also include my family for their emotional, spiritual, and physical support; with an added word of gratitude to my mother, Ann Meisenbach, who from the moment of his birth, has felt every tear and every triumph her grandson has ever had. Roonie, you are truly the definition of what a grandmother should be.

Acknowledgments

I am also very thankful to my loving, supportive husband, who reminds me on a daily basis that being highly active is a blessing, not a hindrance. And to my daughter, Amanda—girl, you have the patience of a saint.

Most importantly, I am grateful to Brandan for coming into our lives and teaching us all how important it is to live fully in the moment. Brandan, sweetie, truly you set your own spirit free. I was just there to take notes.

Introduction

"THE WORLD IS no longer a safe place for little boys like ours."
The first time I heard this statement I was talking to a mother of a nine-year-old boy who had been labeled as having attention deficit hyperactivity disorder. She had been relating the horrors of her son's first two years in elementary school. I nodded my head in agreement as she spoke. My son had been through the same type of torture. "And frankly," this mother added, "I'm really scared for my son." She looked down as she said it, but when she raised her face and her eyes met mine, I could see that she was scared. The truth is she has every right to be.

Not only has the world become unsafe, it has become downright dangerous for boys as well as girls who have been labeled hyperactive. Every year millions of children are given Ritalin and other psychotropic drugs in an effort to make them less fidgety, less opinionated, more focused, and in general as compliant as possible. Even more children are sent to weekly therapy sessions in an attempt to modify behavior that twenty years ago parents wouldn't even consider abnormal. This trend is scary. In fact, it's terrifying—not only for the children who must endure the agonizing slicing and dicing of their spirited nature, but for their advocates who must hopelessly stand by and watch.

Led by drug companies, with the encouragement of many educators and doctors, we are slowly but surely purging our children of any sort of emotional range. We have reached the point where we no longer have the time, energy, or patience to put up with differences. We want children who are great athletes, perfect students, well-mannered, and if at all possible, good-looking. And if we must forego the latter, we are willing to do whatever it takes to make the first three a reality—including putting our kids on drugs and forcing them to spend endless childhood hours on psychiatrists' couches. Certainly, the world is no longer a safe place for children who are incompatible with society's ideals.

I'm not sure when we, as a nation, officially began the emotional obliteration of our spirited sons and daughters, but I assume it started the minute we realized that we could change their unwanted behaviors with drugs. Although our country was founded by men whose rebellious nature made them heroes, as a modern society we have little tolerance for those who cross the line. Somewhere along the way we began to weed out the ones whom we deemed unruly. This homogenization of our children, so to speak, has continued to spread, and while the ramifications of our psychological cleansing haven't always been so obvious, they're beginning to be. This covert war is quickly coming to light as scores of children are refusing to be medicated into submission and modified into monotony. They are standing up for themselves in ways that are most assuredly getting our attention. They are the defiant children who we are beginning to see and hear about on the evening news. The ones who, even with all the medication and psychologists, refuse to fit into society's ideals. Like the frenzied tiger caught in the net, they are resorting to all sorts of horrific acts in order to regain their freedom.

Yet, in our misguided attempts to correct the situation, we are strategically planning to tighten the straightjacket even more. Stronger drugs, earlier intervention, and stricter rules have all been implemented in order to eradicate the unsavory behavior of children. Zero tolerance has become the slogan for the twenty-first century. But the situation seems to be getting worse. The tiger isn't being tamed; he is simply fighting harder. In fact, one might even say he is fighting for his life.

I believe it is time to draw the line now before things get worse for these children, and for society as a whole. We need to cut the ropes, or at least begin to loosen them a bit, so that our children can regain their dignity and their spirits. Rather than attempting to saw off their pointy edges to fit our rounded world, we need to embrace them and make them feel included. More important, we need to remind ourselves that being different doesn't mean being disordered. I truly believe that the answer to making peace with ourselves and our children lies in our recognition that some spirits are simply born to be wild.

So I have written this book. It comes from my heart and from the heart of my son, Brandan. It is the story of how, with the help of some very devoted teachers, a wild child learned to function in the classroom without medicine and ropes. And it is the story of a very creative and loving little boy who thrived, in his home and in the world, because he had parents and a very enlightened doctor who believed he could. It is a story that I could not keep inside, and yet many times it was almost too difficult to write. For in order to put it down on paper, I had to acknowledge some of the horrors that I had allowed my son to undergo. Still, as hard as it was to write, I know it was and is harder to live. That is why it is a story that I believe has to be told. There are many more Brandans out there who are still living under the notion that they are somehow disordered and "wrong." To these children, and to their parents, I offer this story of hope. The world truly needs to be a safe place for all of our children—not just the "perfect" ones.

Born to Be Wild

1

A Typical Day in the Life of a Highly Active Child

The first bits of morning light stream through the foyer window as I make my way past the maze of toys, up the cluttered stairway, and into my son's bedroom. The house itself is ominously silent, as if it is steeling itself against an imminent storm. I, too, am gearing myself for the day ahead. I move into the dimmed bedroom of blue—navy-blue bedspread, baby-blue walls and border. The color is no accident. I coordinated my son's room this way after I read that shades of blue have a calming effect. It is just one of many misguided attempts to slow down my hyper-kinetic child.

I flip on the light and move toward the bed. Bending under the top bunk, I reach in and pull the comforter off Brandan's slender eight-year-old body. Both of his hands immediately begin to flutter in the air in a fruitless attempt to reclaim the covers. "Time to get up for school," I say, handing him his clothes. Although he chose the jeans and shirt himself the night before, he eyes the garments with suspicion. "Get up," I repeat. For a split second he stares back, unsure of what I am asking.

Suddenly, like a platoon caught off guard during a sneak attack, his brain cells begin to mobilize. Seconds later he is not only up and wearing his pants and shirt, but is motoring down the stairs with lightning speed. I quickly follow with a pair of socks in one hand, a well-worn pair of tennis shoes in the other.

By the time I have made it down the stairs and into the kitchen, Brandan has turned on the television and is engrossed in the latest episode of *Pokémon*. I prepare breakfast and put it on the kitchen table. Next comes the first of what I call the "broken record" commands. "Brandan, come eat your breakfast. Brandan, come eat your breakfast. Brandan, come eat your breakfast." I bark the line until finally, as though he is hearing it for the first time, he gravitates toward the table. For the next few minutes he eats standing up.

As soon as I see that he is actually consuming his breakfast, as opposed to flinging it at the cat, I leave to dress myself. By the time I return to the kitchen, he has finished his breakfast and is either eating peanut butter straight out of the jar with a spoon, making water balloons in the sink, or taking the batteries out of every appliance in the house. I start my second series of broken-record calls. "Brandan, put on your socks and shoes. Brandan, put on your socks and shoes. Brandan, put on your socks and shoes." Brandan, in an effort to comply, grabs his socks and starts to unravel them. There is, of course, a hole in one of them. I glance at the clock to see how much time we have left before we must leave for school. If we have more than fifteen minutes, I will send Brandan back upstairs to pick out another pair. Today, we have only eight minutes to spare. I dart upstairs to retrieve them myself. I know better than to ask him to complete a task in less than ten minutes.

After Brandan's shoes and socks are on, I direct him to the bathroom where we both brush our teeth. Toothbrush dangling between his clenched teeth, he uses both hands to comb his inch-long hair straight up. His laughter at his reflection causes him to spit toothpaste everywhere. I look at him through the spray of toothpaste and saliva on the mirror. His brown eyes sparkle back at me. He is not the least bit concerned about drool or mess, or how much time he has left to get to school. He is caught up in the moment, and this particular moment requires laughter. So I take a deep breath and smile. It is the second most useful tool I have these days. The first tool involves a lot of self-talk-reminders that go something like "it's okay; he's okay; I'm going to be okay." Today, I am less strained. Today, I am determined to live in the moment with my son. So we laugh together for a minute before I hand him a washcloth and direct him toward the door.

We live three blocks from school, but they can be a long three blocks for a child with a short attention span and practically no concept of time. So I drive Brandan to school in the morning and allow him to walk home with his friends in the afternoon. On his way to school he sings his favorite song, which has become a mantra in our house, "bong dig it bong dig it bang de bang diggy diggy." We pass some of his friends, and Brandan rolls down the window and sings out to them. The young boys love the entertainment and wave back. At school I hand Brandan his backpack, and before I have time to say good-bye, he is out the car and halfway into the building. I watch him half walk, half skip, half dance out of sight. My heart breathes and smiles.

But as I drive back home, the smiling stops and the worrying commences. Will Brandan cause a problem at school today? Will he be able to finish his work? Will he disrupt the other children to the point that the teacher will call me? Brandan has been medication-free for three months now, and I have yet to get a call from the school. Still, there are mornings when I am at the end of my rope, and I can't help but know that his teachers must be, too. I say a prayer for them as I pull up to the house, and take a vow that if I should ever win the lottery I will buy them all new cars.

I spend my day working at home, and look up to see that it is almost two-forty-five. Brandan will be home before three. I immediately put away my project and prepare for his arrival. My son's daily homecoming can be likened to that of Fred Flintstone. The peace and quiet is immediately shattered as the front door flies open with a gush, and out booms, "Mo-o-om! I'm-m-m ho-o-ome!" Upon which the dog immediately starts barking and the cat runs for cover. Today is no different. Brandan bursts through the door at two-fifty-nine voicing his presence. The thud of his backpack crashing to the floor echoes his announcement.

By the time I have stood up, he has already retrieved three different food items from the pantry. I begin my third broken-record chant of the day. "Sit down at the table and eat. Sit down at the table and eat. Sit down at the table and eat." My husband, who also works out of the house, walks over to see what the fuss is about. "How was school?" he asks Brandan, who is half sitting, half hopping on the chair.

"Good." Brandan's pat answer for everything is mumbled through crumbs of peanut butter and crackers. My husband continues on his way without blinking at the mess that Brandan is making on the floor. I, too, decide to forgo the lecture on table manners and get my purse from the bedroom.

I have promised to pick up my daughter from school so that she doesn't have to ride the bus home. I am relieved that her biggest problem these days is how to get her violin home and feel obliged to make the ten-minute trip to retrieve her and her instrument. "Watch him," I remind my husband as I head out the door. I try not to imagine what calamity will befall the house while I am gone. Leaving my husband and son alone for any length of time is like leaving Curious George with Carrot Top.

On the way back home my daughter chitchats about the kids at her school. She describes the mischievous behavior of several very active boys in her class and how the teachers react. Middle school teachers are obviously not nearly as tolerant of errant behavior as Brandan's are. I make a mental note of this and pray that my son has miraculously changed by the time he gets to sixth grade.

When we arrive home, I see Brandan standing on the front lawn. He has no shoes or jacket on despite the fact that it is forty degrees out. My husband is nowhere to be seen. Brandan immediately runs to the car as soon as he sees us. I decide to forgo worrying about the jacket and concentrate on the shoes. "Go in the house and put your shoes on," I begin to chant. Brandan immediately interrupts my incantation by asking, as he always does when I am away from him for longer than five minutes, "What took you so long?" I move toward the house, determined to get him to comply. "Go inside and put your shoes on." Amanda ignores our bantering and schleps her belongings in the door. With a quick thank-you and hug, she disappears into her room to begin her homework.

Meanwhile, Brandan has disappeared, again. I go to the front yard and call his name. When he appears from the side of the house with his soccer ball, I tell him, "Go inside and put on your shoes and a coat." He looks at me as though he has heard this instruction for the first time and immediately comes in and puts them on. He asks if he can play at a friend's house and I agree to let him if he will promise to be home in an hour. He wipes his face with his sleeve and slams the door as he leaves. It is quiet again, momentarily.

I immediately pick up Brandan's backpack and pull out the wad of papers stuffed inside. It is Thursday, my favorite day of the week. It is on Thursdays that I get to see that Brandan is actually doing better than I am fearing. I look at the stack of papers and am rewarded. He has made ninety or above on both his spelling and math tests. He has completed all his homework correctly and has received all stars on his behavior chart. I breathe and smile for the third time that day. My smile is short-lived. Brandan comes back through the door. "No one is home," he announces. I suggest that he sit down and start some homework. These magic words send him bouncing up the stairs and out of sight. Not to do his homework, but to be out of earshot of my reminders that he has any.

I gather his papers and decide which ones will go on the refrigerator and which ones will be discarded. I take out a picture of an odd-shaped box and read the words underneath it. It is a description of what Brandan would be if he were a gift. It reads: "If I were a present, I would be a Pikachu for Kara (a girl at his school) and she would open me and hug me and snuggle with me." I am touched by the tender words and wonder if it would be too much of an embarrassment for him if I shared it with Kara's mother. Like everything else he does, Brandan has pursued his crush on this sweet little third-grade girl with enormous tenacity. He has made her gifts, ridden his bike by her house, and made several unrequited gestures of affection. Kara's mother has been understandingly patient up to this point, but I can't help but wonder if Brandan's puppy love has reached the point of stalking. I hang the artwork on the refrigerator and make a mental note to ask him about it later. I wad up the rest of the papers and hide them at the bottom of the trash.

I wonder if I have time to finish the project I was working on earlier. I glance at the clock and decide to start dinner instead. I begin by marinating two steaks. I have just finished reading a book about the relationship between blood types and the food you eat. Brandan and my husband are type O. All type Os are supposed to eat meat. Which is good, because Brandan is big on protein and loves peanuts, meat, eggs, and so on. The only problem is that Amanda and I are type B. Red meat is a no-no for Bs. So I also pull some fish out of the refrigerator. As I turn the fish over in the bread crumbs, I wonder what my grandmother would think if she knew that I cooked two different meals every night just to suit my family's blood types.

The sound of Brandan hopping down the stairs, hitting each step with a loud thump, interrupts my thoughts. He slides along the tile into the kitchen in his stocking feet and stops approximately two inches from me. "I hate fish!" he squeals, pinching his nose with his thumb and forefinger. "Good, because it's not for you," I respond. "It's for Amanda and me." A sly grin crosses his face. "Can I help cook?" he asks. I cringe at the thought, but tie an apron around his waist because I know that his offer to help is a step in the right direction. I make him wash his hands and give him a plate of bread crumbs and fish to batter. He flops the fish over in the tiny flakes with amazing tenderness. I watch him as I make the salad, and I can't help but smile. He is Dennis the Menace at his best. He is both angel and devil, and everything in between.

After dinner, Brandan amazes me again by volunteering to do the dishes. I clear the food from table as he sweeps the plates under the running water and jams them crossway into the dishwasher. I am reminded of a commercial for dishwasher detergent in which a mother brags about how hard her family works to clean the dishes. Meanwhile, the family is loading the dishwasher with plates caked with everything from spaghetti sauce to pancake mix. I know that our detergent is not nearly as credible as the one in the commercial, and I advance on Brandan and inconspicuously begin rinsing the plates before he loads them. He insists on doing the dishes himself, though. Maybe in an attempt to be helpful, maybe in an attempt to avoid doing his homework. Whichever the case, the inevitable finally occurs; the kitchen is cleaned and it is time to go to work.

Spelling is first. Math is Brandan's strong point and so we leave that for last. He begrudgingly sits down at the table and I retrieve a few pieces of paper and a pencil from the drawer and place them in front of him. Tonight's spelling homework involves writing each word three times. There are sixteen words. Brandan makes it to the sixth word before he starts to complain. I allow him a short, five-minute break, which he spends eating. He has gained over ten pounds since he was taken off Ritalin, and yet he is still underweight for his height. I am amazed at the amount of food he can put away in a twenty-four-hour period.

Back to work. Brandan is able to finish the rest of his spelling words with lightning speed. After reminding him to put his name at the top of the page, I bring out his math. Brandan has always been good in math. He was able to recite his multiplication tables before second grade. I watch as he moves through the problems in record time. Unfortunately, half of the numbers are illegible. I make him erase the numbers and start again. He is frustrated at my request but complies.

We save the last part of his homework, reading, for after bath. I begin my last series of chants for the day, "Brandan, start your bathwater. Brandan, start your bathwater. Brandan, start your bathwater." After umpteen reminders, the bath water is finally ready and Brandan slides into the tub.

While he is bathing, I fold a load of laundry and help my daughter with a project she has been working on at school. I can hear Brandan singing loudly from where I am in the kitchen. The words are unintelligible, but he sounds quite happy. However, this is not always a good sign. On a hunch, I check on him. Sure enough, he has poured half a bottle of shampoo into the water and is up to his earlobes in suds. I breathe and smile as he covers the last part of his head in bubbles. "Look, Mom, I'm a cloud!" Bypassing the obvious lecture, I hand him a towel and throw an additional one on the floor to sop up the impending mess.

A Typical Day in the Life of a Highly Active Child

Brandan finally makes it into his pajamas with teeth brushed and clothes laid out for tomorrow. I sit with him on the couch and listen to him read. His freshly washed face is soft and smooth and the fragrant smell of his hair reminds me of all the years that have gone by. He was such a sweet, happy baby. When did I start distrusting my own instincts to let him be who he was? When did I start listening to teachers and doctors that insisted that he needed to be medicated in order to survive in the world? I am racked with guilt for a moment, but am quickly distracted by the fact that Brandan is reading with such enthusiasm. He exaggerates each word and sounds out an exclamation point at the end of every sentence whether there is one there or not. He looks up at me and smiles his scraggly-toothed grin.

After reading, I leave Brandan to his father and spend some much needed time alone with Amanda. She seems to be taking her little brother in stride these days, but I know that she is feeling crowded out, and I spend every spare moment I have with her. Tonight we talk about her future. She is only in sixth grade, yet she is already concerned about colleges and careers. I reassure her that there is time to worry about that later.

As I walk downstairs to collect Brandan, I find myself worrying about his future. What will he be doing ten years from now? What if I'm wrong? What if it was a major error to take him off of Ritalin? For a split second I wonder if we should try medicating him again, maybe this time in small doses. But then I think about the depression and the anxiety and the self-consciousness that comes with being on stimulants, and I dig my heels in even further. I will not, I pledge to no one in particular, put my son back on drugs. I sound like a broken record as I repeat my mantra, only this time I am reprimanding myself.

Downstairs, Brandan has snuggled up on the couch with his father. When he sees me coming, he immediately feigns sleep. I pretend not to notice him and sit down on his legs. He shrieks out in indignation, and we both start to laugh. I pull him onto his feet and direct him up the stairs.

Once in bed, I turn off the lights and stretch out next to him. I'm sure that, upon learning that I stay with my son until he falls asleep, a whole slew of psychologists will line up to tell me just how wrong it is. I have heard every argument against it—from keeping him from ever being able to fall asleep on his own, to socially crippling him. I don't care. This is the most humane way of getting Brandan to relax, and it is a way of keeping us connected. Besides, it is only after the lights go out and the dark and stillness of the night takes over that I am able to find out what is really going on in his head. It is during this short time that I become more than just a mother. I become a confidant. Only then will he tell me that he had a fight with his best friend, or share with me that the teacher complimented him on his work.

Tonight he is concerned about another child at school. He rolls his head slightly to the side and relates how a boy in his class is picking on all the other children. In the stream of moonlight cascading through the window, I can make out the small birthmark near Brandan's left temple. This light brown mark, which looks something like a giant freckle in the shape of angel wings, is the spot where an angel kissed him the second he was born—or so I've told him. I gently trace my fingertips across the outline of these wings, and reassure Brandan that all this troubled boy at school needs is a little love and understanding. Knowing in his heart that I am right, Brandan sighs and closes his eyes, his mouth forming a lopsided grin as he drops off to sleep. Together, we breathe and smile.

THESE ARE THE days of a highly active child. These are the moments that define an accelerated spirit. Though the chapter is titled a "typical day," no day is ever typical. In fact, the above description is not really even typical of Brandan's life. Each day in the life of a child like Brandan is new and different, better or worse, than the day before. Because of all that my son and I have been through, I have learned to expect the unexpected. I have learned to ad-lib my life. There are some days when I feel as though I am a water-skier being pulled by a runaway boat, but I am determined to stay out of the wake and on my skis. I am determined to hang on to the rope that binds us, at any speed. More important, I am determined to keep Brandan's motor running and his wild spirit free.

At the helm of this fugitive, runaway boat that is Brandan's body is a child of God who, when given the right longitude and latitude, is destined for greatness. I believe that his boat, which has the ability to clip along at lightning speed toward anything and everything in life without any judgment as to whether it is good or bad, is really a gift. It is not something that is out of control or disordered.

I believe, too, that although Brandan has been labeled hyperactive, he is really hyper-blessed. For he is an accelerated spirit, and to the accelerated spirit, all is to be experienced, all is to be taken in on the palette of the soul and savored. In his eyes and in his heart, all is infinitely good in God's presence. Because he, and other children like him, experience the world in lightning-bolt fashion, they are able to see and feel and taste the divine presence of God in every living thing, including themselves. It is as though they have a sixth sense that makes them hyperaware of all that has been given to them and to the world, and they are determined to enjoy each and every one of God's fruits simultaneously.

There are, of course, many who will say that I don't know what I am talking about. They will say that I am, after all, just a mother. They will point to the experts who say that children like Brandan are disordered—that they need to be fixed, to be stalled, to be made to slow down. Nevertheless, I know that I am right. It is an instinctual thing. It is as though I am almost able to reach out and touch the unique divinity of Brandan's essence whenever I am within breath's reach of him.

So, I wrap my fingers tighter around the invisible chord that keeps me connected to my son and pray. I know that if I can just hang on long enough, Brandan's boat will slow a bit and I will be able to put my face to the wind without flinching. Although he will never outgrow his impulsive nature, I know that as he gets older he will be able to rein himself in. I can see that already with every year that passes he slows down a notch or two. Soon he will be moving at a pace that will allow me to share his blessings with him. Eventually, I may even be able to catch a glimpse of that distant star he is chasing on his moonlit rides.

For the moment at least, staying on my feet and out of Brandan's wake is not easy. No matter how steadfast I am in my beliefs, no matter how divine the blessings, remaining vertical is still very difficult. Staying connected to Brandan's renegade boat is even harder. I have heard even the most experienced parents say that they find themselves belly up and rope-less after only a few hours with their highly active child.

Fortunately, most parents are able to pick up a few helpful skills along the way—skills that make the dodging of catastrophes a whole lot easier. I have endured a very bumpy voyage with Brandan and have garnered an entire suitcase full. A few of these tricks of the trade were shown to me by other mothers, mainly my own, but most were learned the hard way. Through trial and error, I have quickly become an expert on the erratic, a director of the diverse, a master of mayhem. At the same time I know that I am an authority on no one, not even my own child. I know that there is no one trick that works for all children. There is not a single trick that works for my child all the time. Because the spirit of each and every highly active child is unique, I have learned that I must continue to add to my bag of tricks on a daily and even hourly basis. I know that what worked yesterday may not work today, and what works today may or may not work tomorrow. In fact, when asked how life is in their household, most parents of highly active children will answer, "we take one day at a time." One day at a time is indeed how it should go.

I believe that one thing that should never change, though, is the extra love, support, and responsibility that comes with being the parent of a highly active child. That is why staying connected to the boat becomes the biggest trick of all. Once a parent lets go of that invisible cord, they let go of their ability to influence the direction in which their child is moving. They also let go of all the riches and blessings that go along with the journey. There are many tangible as well as intangible rewards secured to the boat. After all, who else but such a child can perform *Riverdance* faster than Michael Flatley or recite Robin Williams's dialogue from *Aladdin* in under two minutes?

Unfortunately the blessings that define the spirit of a highly active child are frequently overlooked by parents who have become distracted by the growing mob of spectators/experts who are shouting directions from the shore. It is hard to concentrate on the beauty of the scenery or the thrill of the speed when friends, neighbors, doctors, and the little old ladies at the grocery store are constantly screaming for you to slow down, let go, turn left, pull up on the rope. Being constantly bombarded with these negative messages is enough to frighten even the most optimistic parent. If you think that hearing the sideline rhetoric is scary for adults, just think about what it does to the spirit of a child.

Most highly active children are acutely aware of critical remarks from bystanders. They hear the messages loud and clear, even the subliminal ones. I see the look on my son's face when he speeds out of control. No one is more horrified at his actions than he is. But constantly monitoring and worrying about his boat does not make him slow down. It just keeps him from enjoying his childhood. It takes the fun and the beauty and the spontaneity out of his gift, and it keeps his spirit from being free.

I wish I could say that I have always known this. And I wish that I could say that my decision to free Brandan's spirit was a result of some grand epiphany. It wasn't. My ability to seek the divine in Brandan, and to concentrate on his blessings instead of his flaws, came out of sheer desperation from listening to too many bystanders. The decision to free his spirit and accept him for who he is was simply a process that I arrived at when nothing else the experts suggested worked.

The horrendous journey officially started the minute we entered the medical maze, and it ended the moment we walked out of it. In the years in between, I took advice from everyone and anyone who had a suggestion about how to raise a highly active child. I dropped the rope that connected me to my son, and I pulled it so tight that I was practically chewed up in his motor. I tried forcing Brandan right, and I tried making him go left. I also allowed doctors, teachers, and psychologists to out-and-out shut off his motor through the use of drugs and stringent behavior-modification techniques. Not only did the advice not help, but it proved to be quite dangerous.

Eventually I reached the point where I knew that if my son was going to survive with any self-esteem at all, I would have to forgo the advice of all the bystanders. I knew that I was also going to have to disregard the advice of any psychiatrist, psychologist, or other expert who hasn't personally raised a highly active child.

This decision to rely on my heart, my gut instinct as a mother, and the wild yet very intuitive spirit of my child to guide me was not an easy one. In fact, the decision to basically fly by the seat of Brandan's pants was probably one of the scariest decisions I have ever made. Yet, as scary as it was and unconventional as it may sound, it has proven to be quite successful. I am still connected to my son's speeding boat. I am still on my feet. And I am as determined as ever to keep his spirit free.

2

The Label of ADHD

I balance myself on the edge of the chair and trim the corners off the long sheet of sticky, blue paper. I am surrounded by two dozen or so cans of food, various spices, and a sack of flour. Trays of tempera paint, jars of colored water, and three pairs of scissors line the counter across from me. A billion snippets of flowery paper litter the kitchen floor. For some ungodly reason I decided that putting down new shelf paper in the kitchen pantry was a good idea. That was at 10 A.M. It is now 6 P.M. and only seven out of the ten shelves have been papered.

Six-year-old Amanda is quietly playing in her room. Three-year-old Brandan is sitting on the family room floor eating chicken fried rice out of the Styrofoam delivery tray that arrived fifteen minutes ago. I had ordered Chinese food in an effort to have more time to finish laying the paper. From where I stand on the chair, I can see that fried rice was not the best choice. There is little, if any, left in the container.

A few bites may have made it into my son's mouth, but most of it has been ground into the carpet by his kicking feet.

I pull the backing off the sheet of tacky paper and flatten it against shelf number eight. I curse my husband for being late. I curse myself for thinking that I could get this done. By the time I turn around, I see that my son has left the family room. I immediately step off my perch and begin looking for him. I know better than to leave him alone for even a few minutes. What was once the terrible twos has turned into the thundering threes. He is three times as impulsive, three times as mischievous. I must be three times as fast.

I check the backyard pool first. There are three separate locks on the back door, permanent closures on all the windows that open to the backyard, and an added safety gate. We had all this installed, in addition to cabinet locks, stove, oven, and dishwasher protectors, outlet covers, toilet fasteners, and door jammers by Dr. Baby Proofer. It took the technician six hours to "Brandan-proof" our house. And although my husband spent the first week swearing because he couldn't even get a drawer open without first figuring out how to work the safety device, it was worth it—Brandan is not in the pool.

I come back inside and check the front door. The locks are still in place. I am relieved. He must be in the house. I call out his very appropriate nickname—"Scrappy"—but there is no answer. Amanda named him this after the short, scruffy dog on the cartoon show *Scooby-Doo*. The name became even more appropriate after Brandan was kicked out of day care for biting.

My frustration level builds. How can one child be so fast, so mischievous, so difficult, so much trouble? I am racked with guilt the moment the words *trouble* and *difficult* cross my mind. Brandan is not trouble, I tell myself. He is not difficult. He is just different. Boys are different. Boys are supposed to be hyper and inattentive and wild. Since he is my only son, I don't really know this for sure, but it makes me feel better.

I remember that Dr. Baby Proofer said that childhood accidents are most likely to occur in the bathroom, and decide I better look there next. There is no sign of him in either bathroom or my bedroom. However, I find remnants of him in the form of a shirt, underwear, and one sock. Brandan is notorious for taking his clothes off. He has been religiously shedding his garments since he was a year old, and it has become almost impossible to keep him dressed, even in the dead of winter. It's as though clothing is just one more limitation, one more hurdle, one more obstacle to overcome.

I quickly weave back through the living room and into the family room, dodging the scattered piles of ground-in fried rice as I go. I glance into the kitchen. Still no Brandan. The rolls of unused shelf paper on the floor remind me that I am probably never going to get the project finished. Feeling as though I am about to explode, I head toward his bedroom, continuing to call his name. The only answer comes from my daughter. "He's outside."

I look toward his bedroom window, which is half open, and a flash of flesh streaks by. I dash outside to find Brandan motoring down the hill in our front yard. With the exception of his left sock, he is, of course, naked. I make a swipe at him, but he is too quick. He is laughing, now—that mischievous, onerous laugh that I will grow to love and fear in the coming years. It is thirty degrees outside and I am freezing. I scream for him to come inside. But by the twinkle in his eye, I can see that he has no intention of obeying me. He darts down the sidewalk. I follow. With one leap I make another grab for him. Too late. I miss and fall to the sidewalk, skinning my elbows and my pride. I look up to see an elderly couple staring at me and at my nudist son. But mostly at me.

Tears well up in my eyes. My elbows are hurting and I feel terribly inadequate, not only as a mother but as a controlled human being. Brandan looks back to see that I have fallen and stops in his tracks. He stares at me for a minute, and when he sees that I am truly hurt, runs to hug me. I want to spank him. I want to scream at him until my lungs hurt. But I don't. Instead I take one of the little hands that is cautiously guarding his backside and lead him into the house. Seven years later the shelf paper is still not done.

EMOTIONALLY DISTURBED, HYPERKINETIC disorder of childhood, hyperkinetic impulse disorder, minimal brain damage, minimal cerebral dysfunction, postencephalitic disorder, attention deficit disorder, attention deficit hyperactivity disorder.

Over the years, these are just some of the labels that have been pinned on children like Brandan. Starting in 1845 when German physician Heinrich Hoffmann portrayed children with hyperactive characteristics in his stories, to the latest move by the American Psychiatric Association to revise its wording to attention deficit hyperactivity disorder, the race to pin a label on children who are highly active has been fast and furious.

But parents of highly active children will tell you that they didn't need a label or a formal diagnosis to know that their children were different. They knew from the second their children were conceived. These restless beings kicked the hardest and came the earliest. They were not born. They were released—like racehorses shooting from the starting gate.

They were the infants who rolled off the bed and out of our arms. They were the babies who hurled themselves over the sides of the crib, vaulted the gates, and climbed out the window shortly after taking their first steps. They were the toddlers that we never, ever took our eyes off of. Yet, they were the children we were most proud of, and we boasted and bragged about them. They were the subjects of the tales told to grandma. They were the ones that the doctors said were so thriving and alert. It wasn't until they became preschoolers or kindergartners that their accelerated spirits began to alarm us.

The first faint moan of the siren may have sounded with an innocent comment from a grandparent, or maybe a friendly discussion with a preschool teacher about the child's activity level. By the time the spirited child was in kindergarten, the harmless remarks became concerned questions. The concerned questions then became interrogations with queries such as

"Has anything changed at home?" Suddenly everyone from grandparents to neighbors converge on the child's behavior and compliments of being precocious and advanced transform into accusations of being spoiled and out of control.

As parents we knew in our hearts that our children were not really spoiled. Out of control? Maybe. But in a way we honored their spirit to talk out and talk back. We saw in them what we wanted in ourselves, and even though they were becoming increasingly annoying, we knew that they were not the monsters that other people were making them out to be.

We felt obligated to do something about our errant child. Stop him. Tame him. Make him like everyone else. When we sought help, we found it on every corner. We were relieved to hear the word *disorder*. We were glad that the entire situation was really out of our hands. People were no longer accusing us of bad parenting. They were sympathizing with our plight of having a child with a "disorder."

In many ways, labels are wonderful things. They help us sort, categorize, define, and identify. They help us figure out what is what and simplify our lives. This simplicity and certainty makes our lives more comfortable. Once something has been labeled we know how to respond to it. We know what to expect. Many times we don't even have to think to act or interact. We only have to react.

Parents and teachers are notorious for labeling children. There's the smart one, the creative one, the shy one. The angel, the bully, the class clown. This classification system allows us to quickly and efficiently discipline children. We don't have to figure out who is in the wrong when Susy and Billy are fighting, because we know that Susy is the shy one and Billy is the bully. Generally, the labeling of people, especially children, makes life much easier.

So, in the beginning, when a child is relatively young, it is easy for parents to go along with the label of being disordered. Having a label eases the burden of raising a child who is impulsive, inattentive, and different. It makes things simple when doctors pronounce that a child has a chemical imbalance. It produces a reason to the very complex rhymes that make up the personality of a highly active child. Parents no longer have to feel inadequate about their parenting skills. Their child has a disorder, a physical reason he can't behave. In many ways the label makes parents feel less responsible for their child's errant behavior.

The accelerated spirit does not gracefully accept labels, though. It is not one that allows for simplicity and categories and definition. In fact, by its very nature it is limitless and irrepressible. There is a wilderness in all accelerated spirits that simply cannot be tamed. You can attempt to label highly active children or categorize them, but you cannot take the wilderness out of their souls. They are the spirits that must go nude in the dead of our winter. They are the children who simply cannot be clothed in society's ideals. You can chase them down, you can continue to dress them in appropriate attire. You can even put up barriers and locks and other devices to keep them fastened in a controlled environment. Sooner or later they will rebel.

As convenient as labels are, they have a way of backfiring with a vengeance. Never is this more so than with the labeling of a child who is highly active. Maybe the child rebels because he knows in his heart that he is not diseased or disordered, only different. And different in a way that will be a blessing, not a burden. Or maybe he revolts because he senses, as all enlightened souls do, that it is the world that is too slow, not he that is too fast. Whatever the reason, the highly active child rebels. Whether it is through an opened window or through an opened heart, he simply will not remain confined for very long.

This unexpected mutiny brings about an even greater panic in the adults around him. The gates and locks are not working. The comfort of having a label is not helping. People are still pointing and staring. Soon, parents are doubting their ability to cope, and more horrifically, they are doubting their child's ability to cope. More stringent measures are taken. Bigger gates, stronger locks, and more severe labels are used. Despite the escalation, the highly active child's behavior often becomes worse, not better. Anxiety levels of the entire family rise, and behaviors that could probably be redirected or tolerated are magnified to the point of becoming unmanageable.

Unfortunately our society adds to the hyperbole by attempting to strong-arm the irregular-shaped star of accelerated spirits into round slots. Schools and teachers begin to buff away at the sharp edges of the child in an effort to "civilize" him. Grandparents and friends continue to push the issue of manners and proper behavior as though being pointy in a round world is an unforgivable atrocity. Psychiatrists, psychologists, and drug companies unmercifully saw off the sharp edges through unnecessary drugs and stringent behavior-modification techniques. Parents' doubt in themselves and even their child, mixed with guilt and, more important, with fear, starts the steamroller of destruction, and the road to fix what's wrong begins to widen.

If I could go back in time, I would allow Brandan to retain his asymmetrical shape. I would remove his label. I would open all the windows and allow him to run nude in the open air in the dead of winter. Even if it meant the whole neighborhood gawked. I would welcome his sharp, pointy edges into my rounded world. I would help him hide from the people who wanted him to be round and clothed in the appropriate attire.

However, that wasn't the road I took. Like most women of my generation, I looked to the outside world to define what type of mother I should be. I was the last person I trusted when it came to raising a child with special needs. So I turned to doctors, educators, books, and labels, and I continued to fret about what the neighbors thought. I sought out experts and sympathy. I not only allowed the label of attention deficit hyperactive disorder to be pinned on Brandan, I actively lobbied for it.

3

The Medical Maze

In the five minutes my son and I have been in the tiny room, he has torn the paper from the examining table, opened and slammed the door no less than a dozen times, and ransacked the latex finger cots. Brandan hates small rooms. I hate them even more. I try reading, rocking, and bouncing him on my knee. I have also tried singing— a talent that only he can appreciate. It is no good. He is a madman in his efforts to escape. Finally the pediatrician comes in. She is smiling, as always, and I feel relieved to be in her presence. She is an expert who most assuredly will be able to find out what is wrong.

My hopes plummet when, after examining Brandan, she cheerfully announces that he is a perfectly healthy three-year-old. That is not what I was hoping to hear. If he is perfectly healthy, why do I feel like I've been hit by a train? I am exhausted from being with him. The pediatrician smiles understandingly as I recant how frantic our days are. I tell her how he was asked to leave preschool. I tell her that the teachers say he has something called ADD. "He does seem especially busy, but I don't think there is anything we can really do now," she says. "Let's watch him and if he is still having a hard time in a year or two, I'll refer you to a specialist."

I do not want to wait a year or two. If I don't find some help soon, I may not live a year or two. I decide to take Brandan to a pediatric neurologist. After a thorough examination, the neurologist explains that Brandan has ADHD— attention deficit hyperactivity disorder. I am relieved that not only is there a medical explanation for my son's behavior, but there is a pill to make him normal. If only I had known before. The neurologist explains to me that the pill will not cure Brandan, only make it easier for him to concentrate. He also mentions that although this drug is not normally given to children under age six, he is prescribing it for Brandan because Brandan is an extreme case. I gratefully take the prescription and put it in my purse. Although I am excited about the fact that the medicine can help my son, I want to do some research on this pill called Ritalin.

It seems that most of the medical community believes that hyperactivity is a neurological disfunction. The truth is that no one knows for sure. From my reading I am impressed with how magnificently orchestrated the brain is. I read about the web of interconnecting networks consisting of nerve cells and synapses, and about how nerve cells are able to communicate with each other through electrical impulses that send chemical messengers from one cell to another. I learn that these chemical messengers are called neurotransmitters and that although there are more than forty of them, doctors have narrowed down three that they believe directly affect the behavior of ADHD children.

It appears that these three neurotransmitters, serotonin, dopamine, and norepinephrine, like all the neurotransmitters, must be in balance with each other, and that even a slight imbalance can wreak havoc. Everything from stress to a major illness can cause an increase or decrease in the level of chemicals. Furthermore, not having the right amount of each transmitter leads to changes in mood, behavior, and personality. It seems that an extreme imbalance in the neurotransmitters are at the root of schizophrenia, aggression, depression, and hyperactivity.

Feeling quite knowledgeable, I reassure myself that Ritalin will be the magic bullet for Brandan. Still, there are a few nagging questions that keep me from filling the prescription right away. If no one has been able to measure the average amount of neurotransmitters in the brain, how do we know how much dopamine, norepinephrine, or serotonin is too much or too little? If every brain is different, who says what is the right amount? How is normal measured in the medical community? How does a physician determine if a child's brain is atypical? How does he or she determine that the brain is not making enough of one of the neurotransmitters?

I decide to do some more research. I look at the use of PET (positron-emission tomography) and other brain-imaging systems and how they are being used to diagnose ADHD. I also come across the statement that most physicians' diagnoses are based on behavior. I ask myself if Brandan's behavior could possibly be within normal boundaries. Since I am not sure what the normal boundaries are for a three-year-old boy, I assume that the doctor thinks they are not. I finally talk myself into getting the Ritalin and make the trip to the pharmacy.

Lesson one: The prescription must be filled within seven days. I head back to the neurologist, get a new prescription, and then return to the pharmacy. While I am waiting for the pharmacy to open, I walk around the store. By the time the pharmacist arrives and I have waited my turn to see him, I have only the top copy of a two-copy prescription. Lesson two: Ritalin is a serious medicine, a schedule II drug, and cannot be filled without both copies of the prescription. This is going to be a lot more complicated than I had anticipated. I spend the next half hour retracing my steps in the store before I finally find the second copy. In hindsight, I wonder if this wasn't a sign that what I was doing was terribly wrong.

At home I take out one of the little yellow pills and hand it to Brandan. He is able to swallow it with relative ease. I watch him closely. He slows down a little bit, but no major change occurs. The next day I give him another pill. I notice that he is especially sullen and quiet, but he functions so much better. He sits still and works a puzzle. I am ecstatic. It is working! Brandan is no longer hyper, and he is keeping his clothes on.

We decide to enroll him in a private school, and for the first few years things are okay. Then the problems start. With every little pill comes anger, depression, and emotional outbursts. The medicine is lasting for shorter periods of time. The teachers are complaining. Brandan is complaining. No one is happy. The dosage is increased and the time span between the pills is decreased. Although most days Brandan looks like a zombie, the teachers are finally pleased. They send a note home saying that he is a "model" student.

We decide to continue with the Ritalin, and Brandan does okay for another year, but then things begin to deteriorate, again. Brandan is taken off of Ritalin and put on Adderall, another stimulant. Just when I think things can't get any worse, they do. Adderall magnifies his anger and depression. Additional drugs are added. Dosages are increased. Psychiatrists and therapists are brought in. I can see that my son is ready to jump out of his skin. I am horrified. I am frozen in fear. My husband and I want to take Brandan off of his medicine, but are afraid to go against the physicians and teachers. Brandan finally makes the decision for us when he has a major outburst at school, throwing chairs and books, and threatening to run away. Suddenly, everyone, including the educators and doctors, are forced to stop and listen to what his body has been screaming for the past five years.

The drugs are stopped cold turkey. Unfortunately, the road off of them is just as difficult as the road onto them. It takes Brandan over a year to recover emotionally. I am convinced that I have fried my son's brain. I later read that drugs like the ones he was on should never be stopped cold turkey. Brandan no longer trusts anyone in a white coat. I feel the same way.

But trust we must. For every misguided doctor, there has been one who I know truly cared. How, I wonder, did we get so caught up in this medical maze? How did I become so readily convinced that being normal was so essential to my son's well-being that I was willing to gamble with his brain? And more importantly how did these doctors get so railroaded into believing that normalcy can be purchased in a pill?

EVERY DECADE OVER the past century has brought new and different theories, diagnoses, and treatments by the medical community in the race to prove that highly active behavior is a medical illness. In the early 1900s, British pediatrician George F. Still claimed that hyperkinetic children had a disturbance that was biologically based. In the 1920s researcher F. G. Ebaugh decided that these children needed intervention. In the 1930s Dr. Charles Bradley began treating hyperkinetic children with stimulants. In the 1940s and 1950s, additional research was performed on brain-damaged soldiers to detect whether the brain damage had a correlation to behavior changes. In the 1960s the American Psychiatric Association jumped on the bandwagon and developed its own label— hyperkinetic disorder of childhood. The 1960s also brought about the use of Ritalin to treat highly active children. In the 1970s the medical community decided that attention and impulsivity problems were at the root of the behavior problems associated with hyperkinetic children. Starting in the 1980s the American Psychiatric Association began to revise its label to reflect several variations of attention deficit disorder with hyperactivity. Its latest versions are attention deficit hyperactivity disorder and undifferentiated attention deficit disorder.

Despite all its name changes, attention deficit disorder, with or without hyperactivity, remains the most commonly diagnosed childhood anomaly. Its treatment often involves a long and complicated trip through the medical maze. Yet there are many who steadfastly believe that there is no such disorder at all, only a difference in thought process. Books from *Ritalin Is Not the Answer,* by David B. Stein, and *The Myth of the A.D.D. Child,* by Thomas Armstrong, to *The Edison Trait,* by Lucy Jo Palladino, have become quite popular. In fact, despite the increase of drugs to treat ADHD, there is also a rise in the number of children's advocacy groups who are taking a stand against medical intervention to treat it. So, after a century of exploring and studying highly active children, the question remains: Is ADHD a physiological abnormality or not?

It depends on whom parents ask. And the diagnosis and treatment that a child receives also depends on whose advice is solicited. As a whole, the medical community, which in this day and age of scientific breakthroughs is usually the first place parents turn, says that yes, ADHD is a physiological abnormality. They say that highly active, inattentive, and impulsive behavior is a result of a chemical imbalance that is most likely caused by insufficient amounts of the neurotransmitters serotonin, norepinephrine, and dopamine. Its treatment, therefore, involves the use of drugs that work to increase the availability of these neurotransmitters.

Of course, no parent wants to put his or her child on drugs, but in desperate times, accepting the medical community's explanation for the child's behavior is sometimes the easiest path to take. I'm not sure when the increasing need to fix everything with a pill began, but I believe it started the minute we, as a society, put blind faith in doctors. Physicians have become the demigods of the twenty-first century. All too often their opinions are revered without question, especially when it comes to children. Their position is further elevated by the boost of drug manufacturers who cater to their prominent status by pushing the latest remedy. While I have known a few doctors in my time who actually did deserve this sort of acclamation, as a general rule, physicians are human and humans are fallible. This goes for teachers, too. Although educators are not officially a part of the medical community, over the years they, too, have achieved a status that has allowed them to have the last say on whether or not a child should be put on drugs. Of course, for litigious reasons, teachers are not allowed to officially recommend a specific drug, but they frequently make suggestions that encourage the use of medication to solve a child's problems at school. Faced with teachers, doctors, and the ever-strengthening shove by the drug companies, parents feel that they have no choice but to seek medical intervention.

Another reason parents are so easily lured into accepting a physiological explanation is that they are afraid not to.

They are frequently led to believe that without medical intervention their child won't be able to learn, or that he or she will have trouble socializing. The fact that children who are impulsive are more likely to engage in dangerous behavior may also weigh heavily on their minds. This was certainly a factor in my decision to place Brandan on stimulants. Brandan was always doing something risky. I remember a teacher asking me, "If he were a diabetic, you would give him insulin, wouldn't you?" She made it seem as though Brandan's impulsive behavior was life threatening. And although it sounded plausible at the time, comparing Ritalin and hyperactivity to insulin and diabetes was not only ridiculous, it was insulting to the millions of diabetics who truly need insulin in order to survive. Nevertheless, this teacher's question worked like a charm. Not only did I continue giving Brandan the Ritalin despite the horrific side effects, but I allowed the doctor to increase the dosage.

This sort of backward thinking, of increasing the dosage if it isn't working, instead of removing the drug, is part of the grand illusion of being trapped in the medical maze. Once parents have ventured far enough into its twisted turns and shadowy paths, they lose their perspective. And if their child begins to experience serious side effects, life can quickly become a frenzied nightmare as they make a mad dash for the exit. However, much to their horror, instead of making a hasty departure, parents find themselves met with dead ends and detours. Like any maze, the only way out of the complex mess appears to be to forge ahead. Higher dosages and additional drugs are prescribed, which only serves to send the child and parent deeper and deeper into the maze. Eventually, the only way out is to tear down the walls, which sometimes means a stay in the hospital so that the child can detox under medical supervision.

The attraction of the medical maze and its ensuing complications are not the sole fault of the medical community, nor should the entire blame for turning ADHD into a physiological abnormality be placed on physicians, teachers, or drug manufacturers. Many times parents are the ones at fault. Many mothers and fathers actively seek out a physician's help, and not only willingly accept a prescription, but demand it. They do this for several reasons. Perhaps the most unsavory one has to do with pride. And while vanity seems like an absurd reason to employ the use of drugs, the fact is that having a medical diagnosis to explain away a child's wild behavior is comforting for parents. It removes the uncertainty and guilt that comes with parenting a child who is different. At the same time it brings about an odd sort of sympathy for both the parent and the child. Parents also employ the use of drugs out of fear; fear that their child will be different if they don't, fear that their child will not receive an adequate education, and most of all, fear of what their child's future will look like if they don't.

Another reason parents enter the medical maze is that the drugs used to correct the unwanted behavior work. The undisputed fact remains that children who are given stimulants are more attentive and less impulsive. Highly active children stop acting highly active when they take the prescribed medicine. At the time that I started giving Brandan Ritalin, it did seem like the magic bullet. It slowed him down. He minded better and stopped engaging in risky behavior. The only problem was that although I was told that Ritalin did have a few side effects, such as causing a low appetite and restlessness before bedtime, I was never told that it might also cause him to be agitated, depressed, and moody. I was never informed about the trade-off I would be making by giving him the pills.

In looking back at my son's frightening journey through the medical maze, it doesn't make me feel any better to say that his doctor should have known not to put him on drugs. It doesn't make me feel better to say that the teachers encouraged me to do so. The truth is that I should have known better. I should have backed out the moment I realized just how bad things were getting. I should have let go of my pride, my fear, and ignored the opinions of the teachers and the willingness of the doctors and just stayed out of the maze altogether.

But I didn't. And there are many more parents like me who find themselves standing at the grand entrance to the medical maze with nowhere to go but in. In most of these cases parents have reached the end of their rope and simply don't feel as though they can survive another day with their child. In other instances, they find themselves so confused by all the medical jargon, controversy, and general hoopla that they unwittingly wander inside.

Although it may seem like a big leap, the first step into the medical labyrinth is usually a small one and involves something as simple as seeing the pediatrician. Seeing a child's doctor is a positive step once parents have come to the conclusion that help is needed. In order to actually make a diagnosis of hyperactivity, other reasons for a child's behavior will be ruled out. There are many physical ailments that affect a child's conduct and make him appear to be overly active. Some of these illnesses include hypothyroidism or hyperthyroidism, fluctuations in blood sugar, iron deficiency, seizure disorder, mental intoxication, hearing or vision loss, and chemical sensitivities. Emotional and mental illnesses such as depression, anxiety, and bipolar disorder can also reproduce some of the same symptoms. Once all other causes for their child's whirlwind behavior have been eliminated, parents are then forced to make a commitment to either move forward or back out of the maze altogether. This is where the slope gets slippery.

If they decide to continue on, the next step most parents make is to employ a physician who specializes in highly active children. In seeking the help of this specialist, it is important for parents to find someone who has several different ways of working with a child who is extremely active. Ideally, parents should look for a doctor who isn't out to tame the tiger, but there to support the family in a way that allows the child's spirit to remain free. This means making sure that the specialist's idea of support isn't found in a bottle of pills.

The problem with finding a specialist is that there are at least a half a dozen types of physicians who claim that highly active children fall under their expertise. This ongoing race among doctors to use their own area of proficiency to make a diagnosis reminds me of a theory that states that if you go to a podiatrist, be prepared to be diagnosed with a foot problem; if you go to an ear, nose, and throat doctor, be prepared to be diagnosed with an ear, nose, or throat problem. I can't help but believe it's especially true when it comes to something as controversial as ADHD. Each specialist, from the homeopathic doctor to the psychiatrist, will provide a prognosis and a treatment that conforms to his training and expertise. And parents should keep this in mind when deciding who to trust.

The two most notable types of physicians who work with highly active children are neurologists and psychiatrists. Neurologists specialize in problems of the brain and nervous system. Psychiatrists are proficient in mental and behavior disorders. I initially sought out a pediatric neurologist in trying to find help for Brandan because I didn't want the stigma of having him go to a psychiatrist. Later, because his school work was deteriorating at such a rapid rate, I did seek out the help of a psychiatrist. Unfortunately, this doctor only made things worse by adding additional drugs. Eventually I was able to find another psychiatrist, though, who was able to help. This second psychiatrist not only stabilized my son emotionally, but he was the first physician to actually stand up and say that putting Brandan on any type of drug was not a good idea. In fact, he flat-out plucked Brandan from the medical maze and set us on a drug-free path to freedom. He was, in my eyes, a godsend. And not only have I put him at the top of my list of people to buy cars for should I win the lottery, but he has inspired me to start a whole new list of people I will buy houses for.

In addition to making sure they have a reputable guide, there are several other important factors that parents must remember when making their way through the medical maze. The first is that they have to be vigilant. Parents must take an active role in knowing about the drug or drugs that are being prescribed for their child. Reading from the medical texts is not enough. In order to be truly informed, they also need to network with other parents. Finding a support group, even at the initial stages of diagnosis, is very important. Many times parents can forewarn other parents about the potential side effects of a drug that the physician has failed to mention. Other parents are also excellent guides for helping others find their way out of the maze.

The second thing to remember when deciding to use any drug, herb, or homeopathic medicine, is to stick with the lowest dosage available. Although most parents and teachers are under the impression that increasing the dosage will help a child even more, many times this increase has the opposite effect. The higher the dose gets, the deeper a child gets into the maze. Keeping the dosage low will help back a child out of the dead-end pathways faster and easier if serious side effects should start to occur.

It is also important to keep in mind that with every drug that is added, the medical maze becomes more and more complicated. Although some doctors believe that it is acceptable to add one or more drugs to offset the side effects of an initial drug, I believe in most cases it is nothing short of absurd. Especially when the first drug is being used to treat something that is non–life threatening. In many cases lowering the dose of the first drug often decreases unwanted side effects, and eradicates the need for the second drug altogether.

Finally, if at any point along the way the child's behavior or mood gets worse, parents should enlist their doctor in helping them take a step backward instead of forward. Stimulants and other psychotropic drugs that are used to treat highly active children need to be decreased slowly, and the decrease should be done only under the care of a physician. A child should never be removed from them cold turkey.

Overall, I firmly believe it is better to stay out of the medical maze altogether. No matter how safe pharmaceutical companies and doctors claim psychoactive drugs are, the fact remains that no one knows for sure how they will affect any one child. And the trade-offs that may occur, such as anxiety, mood swings, and depression, are usually more than a parent bargained for.

4

The Search for Alternative Treatments

I am standing in the middle of the kitchen trying to explain to four-year-old Brandan why he can't have any Wheat Thins. He is either not listening or doesn't care. Or more likely, just doesn't understand. Neither do I, really. But I am determined to try. "They're healthy," he reasons, clutching the box to his chest. I try again to explain. "But they are not on your elimination diet and that means they are not good for you."

My seven-year-old daughter overhears the conversation and asks what elimination means. "It means 'to get rid of,'" I say, as I attempt to wrestle the box out of my son's arms.

I have just spent the last three weeks reading anything and everything that has to do with highly active children and food. Most of the information seems to point to grains as the offending source, so I have excluded all wheat products from Brandan's diet in an attempt to "eliminate" his hyper behavior.

So far it is not working. Brandan has been without wheat/grains for a week and has not slowed down a bit. At four he is not only stronger than I am, but faster. He darts around the kitchen table and squats on the floor behind a chair. I am frustrated, but determined. I drop to all fours and crawl to him. He slinks by me, spilling a trail of Wheat Thins along the way.

I scramble to my feet, corner Brandan by the refrigerator, and confiscate the box. "No, no, no!" I say. Brandan immediately picks up the broken bits of crackers from the tiled floor and plops them into his mouth by the handful. My husband suddenly appears. "Hey, what happened to my Wheat Thins?" he asks. I shove the empty box at him and storm out.

It has been a long day, a long week, and a long four years. I am exhausted from my search to find a remedy that will slow down my son. I retreat to my room and drape myself vertically across the unmade bed. Lately even the simplest of household tasks have taken a backseat to my quest to find a brake for Brandan's accelerated energy level. I lie flat on my back and gaze up at the ceiling fan, going around and around and around. Brandan and I are like the rectangular-shaped blades that swirl overhead, a constant motion of going, going, going, only to end up at the exact same place.

Now that hyperactivity is an official diagnosis, there is no shortage of holistic, psychological, and medical antidotes for the disorder. In a mad dash to fix Brandan, I have tried every single one. However, with the exception of

Ritalin, none of them have had a noticeable effect. And while Ritalin does seem to have the desired outcome of slowing down my son, it also has some disturbing side effects. It not only subdues him physically, it subdues him emotionally and spiritually.

I reposition myself on the bed and try not to think about Brandan's behavior. I can't. Like the fan, my mind is in perpetual motion, desperate to keep churning out possible solutions. I know that the little yellow pill is not the answer. Yet, without it, I can't control Brandan. This thought immediately makes me feel guilty and panic-stricken. What kind of mother needs a pill to control a four-year-old? Although I had never thought about whether or not I could control Brandan until the psychologist had brought it up in our last session, having control has now become a major point of contention for me.

"It is essential that you gain control of him now, before he becomes defiant," the psychologist had warned at our last meeting. He had a name, another label, for the anarchy—oppositional defiant disorder; ODD for short. He claimed that teenage boys, especially those with ADHD, are at high risk, and that if I didn't want Brandan to become defiant later on, I had better learn to control him now, while he was still young. I couldn't help but wonder who came up with this disorder. After all, aren't teenagers supposed to be defiant and oppositional? Although the ODD label sounded utterly absurd to me, I was too embarrassed to question the psychologist further. He was one of the most renowned ADHD experts, came highly recommended, and had a ridiculously long waiting list. I didn't want our sessions to be bumped, so I had listened intently and had followed his directions closely.

"Tell Brandan to pick up his toys and come here," the doctor had instructed. I immediately dispatched the command to Brandan, who was engrossed in the corner of the room with two toy trucks and a bucket full of plastic green army men. As predicted, he either ignored me or didn't hear me. I pretended that it was the latter, cleared my throat, and restated the order a little louder. He looked up and smiled sweetly, but continued to play.

The doctor didn't look a bit surprised at Brandan's lack of compliance. In fact, he had a sort of self-righteous smirk on his face. As I started to repeat the request a third time, he held up his hand for me to stop, and with the heavy sigh of a man who seemed almost bored with the responsibility of being the designated taskmaster, said, "Go and get him, Mrs. Boylan." I did as I was told, dragging a very unhappy Brandan back to the couch by his heels.

I was then instructed to sit on the carpeted floor and wrap my legs around Brandan's waist and my arms around his arms in what was called a basket hold. Because I was wearing a skirt, it was a maneuver that was not only humiliating to Brandan, it was humiliating to me. At first Brandan thought being embraced in a human straightjacket was a game. He laughed for a moment and pretended to struggle. However, he quickly grew tired of sitting in the distorted position and became like a rabid animal in his determination to free himself.

I, too, grew increasingly uncomfortable and looked up at the psychologist, who was perched above me in his chair like the Cheshire cat. He pressed his lips together and shook his head. "Four minutes." It had already seemed like ten, but I was intent on showing this expert, and myself, that I was indeed in control, and continued to keep my limbs wrapped tightly around my now hysterical son. I tried to distract myself by thinking about more pertinent things, like whether or not my underwear was showing. Meanwhile, Brandan continued to cry and scream and plead for me to release him. The tiger in him pulled, pushed, kicked, and finally began to bite. It was all I could do to remain in a semi-vertical position. Together we teetered back and forth on the floor like a two-headed wobbling Weeble. At some point I lost both my shoes and a small fistful of hair.

We remained like that, disheveled and humiliated, me tugging on my rising skirt and Brandan wailing in my octopus-like grasp until, mercifully, the remaining minutes were up. Once I finally released my grip, my whimpering child darted to the office door and pleaded to be let out. The horrified expression on his face remains fresh in my mind six months later.

I lie on my bed and shudder at the thought of that look. It was a look of betrayal, of terror. It was a look that begged the question, "What have these two evil beings done with my real mommy?" Expert or not, we can't go back to that psychologist again. I am sure that another session would cause both of us to develop post-traumatic stress disorder, if the first one didn't already. This was my first experience with a psychologist or a psychiatrist, and I'm not sure I want to try again. How can strong-arming someone, whether they are three or thirty, really make them comply? Shouldn't a child conform out of a sense of love and respect, not out of fear? Although I have rarely spanked Brandan, I can't help but think that a smack on the bottom would have at least been more humane than what I had put him through that day.

Truthfully, though, I have done other things that now seem equally as insane as that day in the psychologist's office. Like the time I spent almost a thousand dollars and several days at an environmental health center having Brandan tested for allergies. Or the time I painted everything in his room blue, because I had read that the color has a calming effect on children. The list goes on and on.

As I continue to watch the fan spin above my head, I feel myself growing angry at the thought of spending so much money and time on cynical psychologists, difficult diets, and ridiculous red herrings, only to be no closer to slowing Brandan's body down than when I started. I can't help but wonder what parents with children like Brandan did before there were all these interventions.

As if on cue, Brandan opens the door to my bedroom. He is suspiciously quiet. He slinks over to the bed and climbs aboard. Throwing his left leg over my torso, he straddles my midsection. He turns his hand over to display a tightly clenched fist. Slowly the fist opens up for me to see inside it. In his sweaty palm are the crumbled remains of a single Wheat Thin. "Here, Mom," he says. "I didn't eat it."

As he says this, a saliva-drenched spray of tiny crumbs flies into my face. He smiles sweetly. I smile back.

ELIMINATING CERTAIN FOODS, yeast control, feng shuing his room, attaching magnets to his shoes, adding vitamin supplements, sessions with psychologists, allergy testing, and behavior-modification techniques are only a few of the dozen or so nondrug remedies I have experimented with over the years in an effort to eradicate Brandan's boisterous behavior. Like an overweight dieter desperate to dump pounds, I have gone through periods of time where I was willing to attempt almost anything. We have used every therapy and fad diet available. Brandan is now eleven, and to this date, nothing has completely eliminated his over-the-top activity level.

Thankfully, though, I have come to my senses and have stopped trying to change my son. After years and years of torturing him and the entire family with my ridiculous remedies, I now realize that there is no cure that treats highly active children across the board, because there is no disease, disorder, or illness to cure. There is nothing pathological to eradicate.

In retrospect, I see that my error has been in attempting to heal Brandan, instead of attempting to guide him. Time that could have best been spent teaching my son how to streamline his energy was wasted trying to crush it. Instead of using those precious years trying to control him, I should have used them teaching him how to control himself. In looking back, I see that I made the classic parental mistake of acting out of fear instead of acting out of love. I let the scare tactics of psychologists and educators force me in the direction of doubt instead of one of trust.

During my pointless quest I wasted many years; years that, unfortunately for both of us, can't be taken back. However, I am fortunate that Brandan is still young. I may have wasted years, but I haven't wasted decades. My time with my son is now spent directing him how to use his gift of being highly active to everyone's advantage. It is also spent trusting that divine order has a special place in both our lives. For I truly believe that God would not have bestowed this type of high-voltage energy on Brandan if He didn't have a great plan, or mission, in store for his life.

Keeping in mind that I am looking for ways in which I can help Brandan harmonize his intense nature with the rest of the world, I have transformed my search for cures into a search for complementary reinforcements. These complementary reinforcements are geared toward supporting Brandan in his mission to take on the world, and are in no way meant to alter his personality or eradicate the traits that come with being highly active. In essence, they are the parenting skills and tools that make my relationship with Brandan more enjoyable for both of us. They are the "tricks up my sleeve" that I rely on when conventional parenting skills don't work.

One of the most effective reinforcements I employ is sleep. Although most people can vary their sleeping patterns by a few hours and still function the next day, highly active children cannot. Having a regular bedtime is essential to their well-being. A lack of sleep not only affects them mentally, but it can physically make them ill. The circadian rhythms of highly active children are so fine-tuned that getting off their sleep schedule for even an hour or two can make the difference between a good day and a horrendous one. In the spring and fall, when the clocks change, Brandan turns from Dr. Jekyll to Mr. Hyde. It takes at least two weeks for his body to adjust. During this time, his grades slip, his eating habits are erratic, and he is generally more susceptible to illness. He is also this way during other times of the year when his bedtime is delayed for more than an hour.

Paradoxically, one of the hallmarks of the highly active child is wanting to stay up all night. This has lead to many battles, skirmishes, and out-and-out wars at our house. Lack of sleep also has a bizarre way of snowballing. When Brandan is overtired, it makes reasoning with him about bedtime even harder. So instead of missing an hour or two one night, his entire sleep schedule for the week gets out of wack. And once that happens it takes a major effort on the part of the entire family to get him back on track. Therefore, I have made a regular bedtime top priority at our house.

Another resource I use is professional counseling. Despite my nightmarish first experience with a psychologist, I have found therapy to be quite useful over the years—not for Brandan, but for myself and my husband. Although I have been told that one-on-one counseling is beneficial for highly active children, I haven't found it all that helpful for my son or for any other spirited child. In fact, many times it is impossible to even get the child to attend the sessions, much less participate in a constructive manner, because highly active children, by their very nature, are inclined to rebel against the rigid structure that is required during these sessions. Furthermore, they are not generally gifted with the ability to communicate one-on-one. Spirited children work best in group settings with lots of stimulation, and sitting through an hour session with a therapist is torture for them. Even if a parent is lucky enough to stumble upon a psychologist who is engaging enough to keep the child's attention for very long, it becomes little more than an expensive play date.

Therapy for an exhausted parent, however, can be very helpful. In fact it can be a godsend if the therapist truly understands the nature of the highly active child, and is willing to outline some ways to help a parent cope. Therapy can also be beneficial in helping parents set long- and short-term goals for their child, and in helping siblings cope with their brother or sister's behavior. Many times all a family needs is some assistance in sorting through the overwhelming stress that comes with living with a spirited child.

In my own experience with therapists, I have found that it is important to be very clear on what it is I want to accomplish. Psychologists, psychiatrists, and social workers come with a variety of temperaments, opinions, training, skills, and fees. Personally, I believe the best ones are those who incorporate spiritual exercises into their practices. Other parents may feel differently, instead wanting a therapist who goes strictly by the book. I also believe it is important to ask about the fees and insurance plans over the phone, rather than waiting for the first session. In the beginning money may not be a problem, but over the long run therapy can become quite expensive.

Above all, parents shouldn't expect therapy to drastically change the nature of their child. Anyone who claims that they can alter a child's personality through counseling is lying. What a good therapist can do is to assist parents with day-to-day problems that arise, remind them that they are not alone in what they are going through, direct them to other specialists, and be a pivotal member of their child's support team as he moves through the difficult stages of his life. It is also important to remember that therapy is a long-term solution, not something that can be accomplished in six or seven weeks.

Another tool that has proven to be quite helpful in slowing Brandan down a bit is the use of vitamins. Like psychotherapy and sufficient sleep, vitamins and other dietary changes will not drastically alter a child's personality. However, they do have a place in helping children who are highly active. It has been known for some time now that a deficiency of trace minerals or B vitamins can have a detrimental affect on the brain and nervous system. Now new studies are also starting to show a link between highly active children and insufficient levels of amino acids and essential fatty acids. Although there is no definite answer from the medical community on either of these vitamins, I believe that as time goes on physicians will eventually come to rely on the supplemental use of vitamins, rather than stimulants, to help children focus.

In addition to employing resources such as vitamins, sleep, and psychotherapy, there are many other alternative treatments such as biofeedback that are being studied. Other parenting tools that I have found extremely helpful include finding a school that is right for your child, staying connected, fostering friendships, teaching self-monitoring and listening skills, and developing an awareness of when to choose your battles, and these are covered in the following chapters. Again, it is important to remember that utilizing these tools will not drastically alter a child's personality. Being highly active is not a disease or a disorder, and it should not be treated as one. Alternative treatments and resources should only be used as a way to streamline a child's energy and soothe a parent's nerves. In essence, they are tools that make being a highly active child in a world of people who are not a little bit easier.

Most of the time, I find that employing only one of these parenting skills is enough to get Brandan and I through the day. Other times I find that I need two or three. Then, of course, there are days when I use every parenting skill on my list, and not a dent will have been made in my effort to streamline Brandan's energy or soothe my nerves. During these times I put the tools aside and let him surge through the currents without a compass, paddles, or a life raft. Still he copes. He finds his way, even if it means going over a waterfall or two.

5

The Educational Maze

I am propped up in bed with my laptop, surrounded by stacks of books, legal pads, wadded-up tissues, various flavored throat lozenges, and a half-empty bottle of NyQuil. I am up to my eyeballs in research for a new project and am determined to finish it by the end of the week, despite the fact that I am running a fever of 102. Just as I am in mid-sentence of typing the first intelligible thought I have had all morning, the phone rings. From the caller ID, I can see that the call is coming from my seven-year-old son's private school, and I answer it immediately.

Brandan's teacher is on the line. Her voice is crisp and formal, and I know immediately that the news is not good.

"Is Brandan sick?" I ask hopefully. Illness is something I know how to deal with; the continuous complaints about Brandan's behavior are not.

"No, he is not ill," the teacher answers. "However, I have brought him down to the office because I want him to explain what he did."

My mind immediately begins to conjure up every possible atrocity that Brandan may have committed in order for his teacher to call me at noon, rather than wait till the end of the day to air her grievances. Did he stab another child with a pencil? Did he throw a chair out the window? My assumptions are interrupted by the sound of Brandan's faint voice.

"Mom," he chokes into the phone. "It's me."

My heart immediately sinks. "What did you do?"

There is momentary silence.

"I ate a chip off of the floor."

I am confused. "A chip? Like a potato chip?"

"Yes." His voice cracks, and I can tell that he is not only humiliated, but scared.

"And then what?" I ask.

"I had to come to the office," he says.

I smile. Obviously, this teacher has never heard of the three-second rule. My amusement quickly shifts to anger, though, when I realize that Brandan is being shamed over such a silly act. "It's okay, honey," I reassure him. "Put your teacher on the phone."

The teacher gets back on the line and I immediately begin to question her. It seems that Brandan has had a bad morning, though I am given no specifics, and the last straw came when he dropped a chip on the floor and then reached down and picked it up and put it in his mouth. I can't believe what I am hearing. I decide not to further humiliate Brandan by grilling the teacher about why in the world she felt the need to call me. Instead I decide to take it up with the school director the following Friday. The director says yes, she heard about the incident, and agrees to a conference with the teacher.

The meeting is held the following Monday in a room with one child-sized table and six miniature chairs. The door is left open, despite my protests, and I can hear Brandan and his classmates in the room across the narrow hallway. We squeeze into the chairs and the director asks the teacher to explain the incident in question.

The teacher, sitting as properly as she can in the tiny chair, begins. "We were walking back from lunch, and one of the children said that Brandan had eaten a chip off of the floor." Her lips press firmly together as she recalls the horrific atrocity. "And when I went back to the end of the line I saw that he indeed had crumbs in his mouth."

The director turns a slight shade of red.

I feel my blood boiling and once again ask that the door to the classroom be closed. I don't want Brandan and his friends to hear us. The director, however, insists on leaving it opened. "It's important that Brandan know we are on the same page." She smiles sweetly and pats my hand.

"But that's just it," I say, pulling back my hand. "I don't think we are. I don't understand why eating a chip off the floor warranted a phone call. Surely Brandan has done other things that are more annoying than that."

"He ate food off of the floor," the teacher reiterates.

"But he didn't literally drop to all fours and lap the chip up with his tongue," I insist. "He picked it up with his hand and ate it." I can't believe that we are even discussing this event, but I am determined not to back down.

"Tell me something, Mrs. Boylan," the teacher queries. "Do you let him eat off of the floor at home?"

I immediately lose any cool I might have had before the meeting, and begin to fling accusations of being obsessive and overcontrolling at the teacher. I threaten to pull Brandan out of school.

"And just what school will possibly take him?" snaps the teacher.

I am enraged and stand up to leave. The director reminds me of how difficult Brandan can be—a mantra she has been reciting since the day he was enrolled. She also says that she has "seen lots of little Brandans," and knows just how to handle them. "Brandan needs lots and lots of structure." She pauses for a moment, and then gets to the real point of the meeting. "Do you think his medicine needs to be increased?"

I know that Brandan does indeed need lots of structure, and that the school does provide it. I also know that teaching a child who is highly active is an exhausting task, so I agree to sit back down. However, I am disturbed that the director is bringing up the medicine issue again. "I think he is taking too much Ritalin, already" I state. "He's sad when he's on it."

The director is obviously upset that I think Brandan is

unhappy and goes across the hall and retrieves him. "Brandan is very happy here," she says, putting him on display. "See."

But Brandan does not look happy. In fact, he looks downright depressed. There is a sadness in his eyes that continues to expand during the remaining two months of school. By the summer he is so depressed that he refuses to go outside and play. The following fall all hell breaks loose at school during a major eruption in which Brandan has to be wrestled to the floor by a male teacher.

Finally we make the decision to take Brandan off the medicine altogether. He is out of school for two weeks while he is detoxed. When he returns, he is just as unhappy as before. Daily calls come from the teacher for me to pick him up. He complains of stomachaches and headaches and earaches. I know what he really has is a heartache.

My husband and I finally come to our senses after having to fetch Brandan from school one hour after we have dropped him off. "We won't be back," my husband grumbles at the teacher. The director calls me that afternoon and agrees with our decision. "We'd love to have Brandan back if you can get him stabilized," she says sweetly. And again, she reiterates that she's not sure what school will possibly accept him.

The next day we decide to enroll him in public school. I am terrified. If he had such a difficult time in a private school setting that was specifically designed for ADHD children, how in the world will he ever be able to conform to a public school? My husband insists that Brandan will be fine. "It can't be any worse than what he's been through." I pray that he is right.

There are twenty other children in Brandan's new classroom. He has never been in a room with more than five at one time. In fact, he hasn't been in any other school since he was three. "Don't worry," the public school principal reassures us during our first meeting. "We won't be calling you." But I am not convinced. What if the director and teacher at the private school were right? How are we ever going to get him educated?

No calls come from the new school. Not that day, not ever.

I am overcome with joy that our lives are back to normal. No more calls, no more planning my day around what's happening at Brandan's school, no more critical remarks from educators about my skills as a parent. I feel more confident about my ability to cope with Brandan's behavior than I ever have before.

At our first parent-teacher conference at the new school we are shown Brandan's desk. Stretching across the two front legs of his chair is a huge rubber band. "That's for Brandan to kick his feet against if he feels jumpy," says the teacher. She has also made other concessions for Brandan's excessive motoring. He is allowed to squeeze a rubber ball during lecture time. He is allowed frequent breaks. He is allowed to be Brandan without being shamed or sent to the office or sent home. He is also assigned a special aide to help him with his work. All this help arrives without even so much as one request from us. I am amazed at how organized and efficient our public school system is when it comes to treating children who learn differently.

I can also see by the way the teacher talks about Brandan that she genuinely likes him. "We have lots of boys who are just like Brandan," she says. Unlike the teachers at his old school, she does not seem stressed or overburdened at all. In fact, she seems to take joy in her job as Brandan's teacher. I immediately fall in love with this woman. By the way that Brandan chirps excessively about her, I can tell that he is also quite smitten.

Every day that goes by Brandan heals a little more. By the end of the school year, he has improved to the point that his doctor says that he is "a new kid." I agree. Although he is still extremely active and distractible, Brandan is less anxious and more confident than he has ever been in his life.

THREE YEARS HAVE passed since Brandan changed schools. During these three years in public school he has come in contact with teachers of various ages and backgrounds. He has adored every single one of them, and they have, in return, given him something that I don't believe he ever received from his private school: the opportunity to be different without being disordered. There have been days when he has been wild, and days when I know that his teachers must have been counting the minutes until school was dismissed. Yet, there have been no calls, no harsh reprimands, and no notes home. Brandan's differences have not only been tolerated, they have been embraced. In fact, not only did he receive student of the week, but he is making As and Bs on his report cards.

In looking back at all that happened with my son, I can now see how imperative it is to find the right school for a child who is highly active. Next to taking Brandan off all medication, changing schools was the best parental decision my husband and I have made. My only regret is not moving him before things reached a crisis point.

I'm not sure what kept me tied to his former school long after it was obvious that it was not the right one for him, but I think fear had a lot to do with it. I knew early on that Brandan needed help focusing, and I felt that putting him in a school that was small and structured was the only answer. He had previously had problems in a day care center with biting, and the fear of not being able to find a school that would accept him left me feeling panicked. The director at the private school played on these fears by reassuring me that she was an expert on handling highly active children like Brandan.

There were problems with that school, even from the start. In fact, the first year was almost as bad as his last. The director called at least twice a week to give me a rundown on what she referred to as "Brandan's antics." These escapades consisted mainly of Brandan's inability to stay in the classroom. I was not surprised at Brandan's desire to wander. Brandan hates confined spaces, and this room was incredibly small. The school was run from an office building, and all the classes were held in tiny offices. There was a three-to-one ratio, which was one of the selling points of the school. Unfortunately, these three children and their teacher were assigned a space that was not much bigger than a walk-in closet. Brandan simply would not stay put. A gate was lodged in the doorway, and that helped for a few days. Eventually Brandan learned to scale it.

Encouraged by the school's director, the neurologist increased Brandan's low dosage of Ritalin. This seemed to help the roaming dilemma, and for years calls from his school were few and far between. His kindergarten/first grade teacher was understanding and supportive. However, once he moved up to second grade, things begin to deteriorate quickly. This older teacher was not as sympathetic. She and the director expected more than Brandan was able to give. Again the Ritalin was increased. This increase, along with the meticulous nature of the new teacher, put Brandan into an emotional straightjacket. I could see the light dimming in his eyes with every passing day that he was in that school.

Like our journey into the medical maze, rather than back out of the predicament, I continued to lead Brandan deeper and deeper into it with every passing day. If I could go back and change things, I would not have allowed a teacher, or a director, to dictate what was wrong with my son. I would also have been more diligent in finding a school that accommodated Brandan's needs in the first place, rather than being so concerned about him living up to the school's expectations. More importantly, I would have immediately pulled him out at the first sign of trouble.

However, I know, too, that while it may be the right thing to do for the child, switching schools is not always possible. Many times parents simply have no choice. If this is the case,

and parents find themselves locked into a school where ar-
chaic teaching methods are still in place, then they must take
the initiative.

I firmly believe that it is up to parents to act as advocates
and to see that the school accommodates their child's differences, rather than expecting their child to fit into an outdated
mold. Children spend more waking hours in school then they
do at home. It is their job. And parents who would not think
of working in a position where they were absolutely miserable should not expect their children to be productive in an
environment where they are not happy. Although there is a
standing belief that children are not supposed to enjoy school,
I have come to understand that children who don't enjoy
school don't learn.

Being an advocate is not always easy. Many public as well
as private school teachers are quite inflexible when it comes
to changing the way they interact with children. They tend to
have a one-size-fits-all way of teaching that leaves little room
for children with different temperaments and needs. Who can
blame them? Teachers are without a doubt the most under-
paid, overworked employees. Their jobs are stressful enough
without having to accommodate children who are climbing
the walls. However, the inhumane way society treats teachers
is a subject all its own, and the role of a parent is to be an advocate for their child, not for the teachers. Therefore, parents
must be prepared to approach the teacher if they feel that
their child is not receiving the education that he or she de-
serves. They must also be willing to support the teacher in her

job by monitoring homework and making sure that the lines of communication remain open.

Before a parent approaches an educator about his or her teaching method, though, I think it is important for parents to understand the chain of command that is in place at most schools. Although the structure of the curriculum and the classroom is dictated as much by the school board as it is by those at the individual schools, it is still best to start with the child's teacher. Sometimes a short meeting is all it takes to make a teacher aware that the child's needs are not being met. Other times, parents may find themselves in a showdown with an obstinate educator. If this is the case, the director or principal of the school should be notified. If the situation is not rectified, then parents should seek help through the school board.

However, parents must keep in mind that if the school board doesn't believe that adjustments should be made for children who learn or behave differently, then they are going to have a hard time trying to convince a teacher or principal to change their methods. Thankfully, the passing of the Individuals with Disabilities Education Act in 1990 that states that accommodations must be made for children with special needs, all public schools must have an IEP (individual education plan) in place for students who qualify in the special needs category. However, the problem with this act is that children have to be labeled by a physician as having an emotional or physical disability in order to get an individual education plan. Hopefully, as society becomes more educated about the different learning styles that children have, all students will be able to receive an individualized plan without having to wear a label.

One of the things I would insist on for Brandan, whether it was found through a new school, or lobbied for in an existing school, is a classroom that is spacious and open. Large, expanding rooms often have a more calming affect on children who are highly active. Previously it was believed that open spaces caused a child to be more distracted. But many children find that the stimulating environment counteracts that distractibility and also gives them room to move.

Another issue I would insist on would be flexibility in the teacher as well as the curriculum. I am certain that as they read this, many educators will immediately begin doing back flips. After all, the consensus has always been that children need to be molded to fit the framework of the school and the teacher, not vice versa. But truly there are too many asymmetrical children who simply will not be cast into symmetrical shapes. And children who will not fit the mold become outcasts. They can rebel to the point of becoming violent. Besides the physical danger of forcing children to become something they are not, do we really want a nation of cookie-cutter kids? If we truly value our individuality as Americans, then we need to mandate that our schools allow our children to have theirs.

Lastly, I would make sure that the highly active child is provided with many opportunities for physical movement, and not just at recess. Experts used to believe that children could not retain information unless they were stationary. It was thought that if a child was moving, he wasn't paying attention. However, some children, especially the spirited ones, actually learn better when they are motoring around. In fact, having to sit motionless for any length frequently causes these children to be less attentive.

In Brandan's public school, his movements are not only allowed, they are encouraged. Devices, such as the rubber band around the legs of the chair and the red hand ball, were brought in to give his hyperkinesis an appropriate outlet. If he is having an especially active day, he is sent on errands such as taking something to the office, or retrieving something for the teacher. I have found that this newfound freedom in movement acts as a release valve that prevents Brandan's energy from becoming bottled up. When he attended private school he used to burst out of his classroom like a time bomb ready to explode at the slightest provocation. Now, his transition from school to home is much smoother, with very few mishaps.

In all fairness, however, I must state that while Brandan had an absolutely miserable time at his private school, I know for a fact that many children are helped by stringent teaching methods. The bottom line in navigating the educational maze means remembering that not all children learn the same way. What may work for one highly active child may not work for another. Although Brandan absolutely thrives in the boisterous classrooms of public school, many children would find it impossible to learn in such an environment.

Therefore, parents need to trust their own instincts when it comes to pinpointing their child's learning style. Despite what the books, teachers, and psychologist say, the truth is that no one knows a child like his parents. While opponents may argue that moms and dads are biased, I believe that any prejudice is offset by the incredible accuracy of parental instinct. I have known from the beginning that Brandan is claustrophobic. Small rooms make him crazy. But since I could find no books that discussed a relationship between confined spaces and hyperactivity, I dismissed the idea. Now that I see how much better Brandan does in an open classroom, I would never require him to learn in such a small, restricted space, no matter what the experts said.

Overall my encounter with the educational process taught me that it is imperative that parents go to bat for their child, no matter how silly or unconventional their premise might be. In the future, as Brandan moves into middle school and high school, I know there will be times when I will have to insist that accommodations be made for his learning style. There may even come a day when I feel that Brandan's needs will be better met by a different school. If that time comes again, I will not be so slow in making a change.

My experience with Brandan's private school also taught me that not only isn't Ritalin the answer, but restrictive ropes aren't, either. Although our retreat from the medical and educational maze was certainly a great starting point in mending his body and his mind, I knew the journey to heal my son was going to have to go much deeper, and it was going to have to encompass more than discarded pills, alternative treatments, and a new school. In essence, it was going to take a concerted effort on everyone's part to look beyond Brandan's highly active mannerisms and into the core of his soul.

6

The Spiritual Nature of the Highly Active Child

I am standing on the front porch in the scorching midday Texas heat watching my nine-year-old son run in circles.

Brandan's bare feet grind into the wet grass as he makes his sharp slippery turns on the front lawn. A muddy circular indentation is forming underneath him. Meanwhile, the garden hose, which he was using to water the lawn, has been abandoned to the sidewalk and is now irrigating the pavement. A steady stream of clear liquid snakes down the cement and into the neighbor's yard.

I have been meaning to tell Brandan to turn off the water and stop making a mess of the lawn, but my fascination with his activity has temporarily silenced me.

Brandan, like most highly active children, always appears to be running in circles. This time his movements seem more concentrated than usual. His head is cocked to the left, his eyes are focused downward, and he seems to be encompassing one particular spot. After observing his rapid, clockwise motion for several minutes, I finally ask him what he is doing.

He slows momentarily, panting out an answer in between breaths. "I'm k-e-e-ping it from jumping away."

My curiosity finally gets the better of me and I stroll out onto the lawn to get a better look. Brandan immediately motions me with his arms not to get too close. I stop where I am and squat on the lawn to see what he is circling. It appears to be nothing. I squint my eyes and look again. Nestled in between the greenery is a large, brownish-yellow grasshopper. Motionless, it appears to be stuck to one particular blade of grass.

Brandan continues to encircle the catatonic insect, making an invisible fence with his locomotive speed. First clockwise, then counterclockwise. Then clockwise again. Brandan is short-winded but determined to keep going. His arms stick straight out to the side. I am not sure if he is holding them out in an effort to stay balanced during his ninety-degree turns, or if he is doing it in an effort to psyche out the grasshopper.

I finally turn off the water, which by this time is not only flooding the sidewalk and the neighbor's lawn, but is also pouring into the street. Curious to know the outcome of my son's quest to keep the insect in one spot, I return to the porch and continue my vigil. I am amazed by Brandan's energy and tenacity in following through on what seems to be such an utterly ridiculous mission. At the same time,

I am also awed by his ability to think of such creative ways to accomplish his objective. I can't help but wonder if the grasshopper is staying put because it is dazed or dead, or because it, too, is awed by the exertion and perseverance of the odd creature circling around it.

The longer I observe, the more convinced I become that Brandan really has hypnotized the insect.

Finally, dizzy from watching him, I order my son to stop. He is all too willing to comply and collapses in a heap on the wet ground. The grasshopper immediately leaps away.

Any other observer would have chalked it up to coincidence. After all, they would say, insects can't be influenced by the intellectual intentions of a little boy. But I know from living with Brandan these past nine years that accelerated souls don't create coincidences, they create miracles. This isn't the first miracle he's produced. My son has been spiritually versed, intuitively blessed, and miraculously gifted since he first popped his tiny head into the world.

Although I crushed Brandan's spiritual gifts for many years through the use of medicine and strong behavior-modification techniques, I now recognize and relish every single one of his miracles. In fact, I have found that since I made the decision to free his spirit from drugs and rigid rules, his ability to create miracles has flourished.

I stand up and walk out onto the lawn to collect my miracle-making son. Just as I get within inches of Brandan, his deflated body springs to life and he begins his hunt for his next telepathic experiment.

ALTHOUGH I FIRMLY believe that the power to perform miracles is available to all human beings, very few of us are able to tap into that ability quite the way that highly active children do.

I'm not sure why this aptitude for producing miracles is so strong in children who have been labeled hyperactive. Maybe it is because these children are the only ones who have the energy to execute the miracles. Or maybe it is because they are so tenacious and hyper-focused that when they sense a miracle in the making, they continue to follow it through to fruition, no matter what outsiders say. Then again, maybe it is because God foresaw the propensity that these children have for getting themselves into trouble, and it is a way of exonerating them. Whatever the reason, their knack for producing miracles is without a doubt one of the most abundant gifts that highly active children possess.

I have seen Brandan pull off exalted feats that would astonish even the most skeptical of critics. He is a deputy of divine intervention, a prime minister of the prodigious, a superintendent of the supernatural. He can visualize and follow through on ideas with such confidence and foresight that I am almost surprised when things don't turn out the way he planned. I have seen this same charismatic trait in every highly active child I have met. For some reason these spirited children are able to climb the mountains and tackle the tasks that other children only dream about. They are the escape artists who make the break with two seconds to spare, the salesman who closes a deal just before the door slams and the athletes who make the goal just as the final buzzer goes off. Without a doubt, highly active children are blessed when it comes to getting what they want.

The innate ability to pull a rabbit out of the hat at the last minute is not always a good thing, however, as it frequently keeps children, as well as adults, from learning from their mistakes. Many times this causes the perpetrator to repeat the same errors over and over because he thinks he can miraculously alter the outcome the next time around. Furthermore, children who are overly confident in their ability to turn the game around in the last few seconds occasionally, and unexpectedly, find themselves facedown on the five-yard line when the final whistle blows.

Nevertheless, the ability to create miracles is still an inspiring and valuable talent to have up one's sleeve when the chips are down and one's back is up against the wall. Actually, the ability to create miracles is just part of the very intense spiritual package that comes with a highly active child. Children who have been labeled as hyperactive are also very intuitive, creative, perceptive, and theistic individuals. They also have the ability to see further down the road then most people would imagine. In fact, one might even say they are the visionaries and the luminaries of the world.

I believe this ability to envision the future comes from the fact that they are always two steps ahead of the rest of us. While most people tend to get caught up in the mire of day-to-day activities, Brandan is daydreaming about Christmas in

July. He is planning his next objective, mentally measuring his next hurdle, or theorizing how he's going to get that castle built in the sky. Two out of three times, that castle not only gets built, but it gets expanded upon.

It was my appreciation of Brandan's spiritual nature that first allowed me to understand that there are many hidden and undiscovered gifts that come with being highly active, gifts that lie buried underneath the rubble of labels and disapproval. For most of Brandan's life I had seen him as disordered. I spent years running in circles, trying desperately to fix him. Even after I reached the point of accepting him just the way he was, I was still blinded by what I saw as his faults. It was only after I realized what a truly gifted child he was spiritually that I knew that I had to do more than just find the right school or stop relying on medications. I was going to have to free his spirit.

Even then, freeing his spirit was an uphill battle. Although I knew in my heart that Brandan was gifted, I still had to fight the many nagging doubts that crept into my mind. Those rigid beliefs about being different, which were unwittingly instilled in me by society, still had a strong hold. These views were even harder to get rid of because they were constantly being reinforced by those around me.

Therefore, I knew that if I was going to truly set Brandan's spirit free, I would have to understand why I had led him down the path I had in the first place. In essence, I was going to have to examine my attitude as well as society's beliefs about what it means to be different.

7

What Society Says About Differences

I am on an airplane, sandwiched in between my twelve-year-old daughter and a twenty-something young man. My daughter is quietly reading. The young man is staring coldly ahead. He does not seem friendly. I take a deep breath and pray that the trip goes smoothly. But as the plane taxis down the runway, the commotion begins.

"Mom! Where's my Pokémon book?" Nine-year-old Brandan is sitting across the aisle with my husband. By the modulation of his voice you'd think we were at home alone in the living room. I dig through my carry-on bag and pass the coloring book to the man next to me. Without turning his head one way or the next, he begrudgingly passes the book across the aisle to my son. Brandan has officially been off of Ritalin for six months, and this is our first plane trip without it. I close my eyes and say a prayer that his interest in the book will at least keep him still until the flight takes off.

No such luck. I hear Brandan squirming in his seat. My husband is trying to appease him by pointing to something out the window. Every muscle in my body tenses. I feel a migraine coming on.

Mercifully, the flight attendant rushes through her speech and within minutes we are taking off. No sooner are we in the air than Brandan unbuckles his seat belt and stands up in the aisle. "You have to stay in the seat!" my husband and I recite in unison.

Brandan begrudgingly plops down and re-buckles his seat belt. I can see from the corner of my eye that the man sitting in front of my son is not happy by the way he turns around and glares at him. I lean across my seatmate and tell my husband to make Brandan stop jiggling the seat in front of him. Without even looking up from the newspaper he is reading, my husband barks, "Knock it off, Brandan!" I don't know what I'm more embarrassed about, my son's behavior or my husband's pointless reprimand.

Brandan begins to whine and fidget. "Just ignore him," my twelve-year-old daughter whispers. She grasps my hand and squeezes it tightly. I begin to fume. I am angry at everyone. I am angry at Brandan for causing a commotion. I am angry at my husband for not coming up with some creative ways to keep him busy. I am angry at the man sitting next to me for not offering to change seats with my son so that he can sit by me. I am angry at my daughter for asking that I sit by her this time (since I sat with Brandan the last time). I am angry at all the passengers who are obviously thinking what a spoiled son I have. Most importantly I am angry at myself for even caring what everyone else thinks.

Once more Brandan unbuckles his seat belt and stands up. "I am going to the bathroom," he announces to no one in particular. I lean around my seatmate and ask my husband to go with Brandan. "He'll be okay," my husband says. I try to relax, but I am terribly uneasy. What if Brandan decides to open the door to the plane, just to see what happens. I try to laugh the ridiculous thought off. After all, the steel door is way too heavy and complicated for a child to open. However, for the next few minutes images of my son being sucked out of the plane continue to plague me. I am relieved when Brandan finally returns to his seat.

Brandan is momentarily appeased when the flight attendant serves dinner. But the moment he is finished eating he begins to squirm again. Like a worm on a hook, he is in agony. I feel bad for him and muster the courage to ask my seatmate if he will please trade places with my son. He begrudgingly agrees. Brandan is relieved to be with Amanda and me, and colors quietly for the next hour.

Toward the end of the trip he begins to fidget again. He lowers and raises his tray a dozen times. He taps his fingers loudly on the armrest. He rummages noisily through his backpack, pushing the seat in front of him back and forth as he does. The elderly lady in the row ahead of us peers at me through the space in the seats. I try smiling at her, but she refuses to smile back. She is obviously annoyed about Brandan's behavior, and I don't blame her. I wish I could take the time to explain to her that Brandan is not disturbing her on purpose, but I know it is pointless. Unless you are the parent of a highly active child, you can never fully understand.

I close my eyes and pretend that I don't see how uncomfortable Brandan's fidgeting is making the other passengers. I momentarily fantasize about standing up and asking if anyone has any spare Ritalin we can borrow. However, the remembrance of that horrible journey on stimulants immediately pops my fantasy like a sharp needle in a bubble. Brandan notices that my eyes are closed and tries to engage me in another game. But I can't open them. My entire body is rebelling as well. I am too tired to read, color, or run interference for my son anymore. I am exhausted from coming up with the two dozen games and finger tricks. My thumbs refuse to participate in any more wars; my fingers refuse to do one more scissor, rock, or paper motion.

Finally, when I feel that at any moment the passengers are going to rise up and throw us overboard, the plane lands.

"YOUR CHILD'S A spoiled brat!" Most parents wince at the thought of these five words being directed at them. I am no exception. Although I would like to believe that I have come far enough in my journey with Brandan that the opinions of bystanders don't have an effect on me, the truth is that they do. What other people think bothers me. When it comes right down to it, like most parents, I want my son to be liked. I want him to have friends. While I tell Brandan that it's not important what other people think of us, the fact remains that we live in a society where the opinions of others do count, especially when it comes to child rearing.

One of the reasons for our reliance on the general consensus stems from a very primitive instinct that has to do with survival of the tribe. For thousands of years, the success and stability of any given society depended on the willingness of its citizens to comply with the rules. Anarchy, and the eventual downfall of the society, occurred when too many people bucked the system; thus any insurrections were quickly crushed. Although the danger of being an outsider is not quite as absolute as it once was, we still depend on society for most of our needs. Being a team player is still important. So we try not to step on too many toes or draw too much attention to ourselves. We continue to sacrifice our needs for the needs of the general population. This sacrifice trickles down to our children as well.

Another reason we are so quick to rely on the opinions and advice of others is that, although we are able to put up a good front, the fact remains that most of us are not prepared for parenthood. It is an area of our lives where we never quite feel up to the challenge. Our insecurities about being a good parent often lead us in search of reassurance. Our doubts also lead us to believe that other people know more about our children than we do. We are all too willing to concede to the opinions of doctors who want to medicate, psychologists who want to analyze, and educators who want to label.

In their defense, I believe that most psychiatrists, psychologists, and educators are simply following the lead of the pharmaceutical companies. Truthfully, being different has become a disorder in our society because the drug market tells us it has. The constant bombardment of advertising by pharmaceutical conglomerates regarding disorders of all types is enough to make even the best of parents reexamine their child's behavior. In essence, pharmaceutical companies are playing on our fears, and it is working. Print advertisement is already under way by these companies pandering a wide variety of stimulants and other psychoactive drugs as quick and easy interventions to fix our problem children as well as our guilt, and I am sure it won't be too much longer before the television networks begin to run similar advertising.

Although for years the consensus was that the best way to curb a child's misbehavior was to ignore it, parents are now being advised by these experts to jump into the middle of their children's lives with both feet, a bag of little yellow pills, and a behavioral straightjacket. Furthermore, a sense of urgency prevails that leads parents to believe that if they don't intervene and do something about their child's behavior (and that something better be drastic and swift), then they are doing a terrible disservice, not only to the child, but to society as a whole.

To complicate things even further, even as we urge our children to conform, in our hearts we still value the renegade. We yearn to be able to color outside the lines, to break a few rules, and to do our own thing. What we really want is a child who is a creative thinker, but not so creative that he won't conform. We want a child who thinks outside the box, but not one who won't fit in it. We want a child who can stand alone, as long as he's not a loner. In essence, what we really want is not a child at all, but an offspring who thinks, acts, and behaves like an adult.

The irony in all this is that the guilt and worry along with the pushing and prodding that most parents go through in an effort to perfect their child is profoundly more damaging to their child's psyche in the long run. Although I truly feel that I am the best parent that I can be, there are many days when I do nothing but obsess about my parental performance. I know that Brandan senses my moods and when he knows that I am worried, he becomes even more anxious. Furthermore, I have noticed that when I am hyper-vigilant about his behavior, it makes stepping out over the line even more tempting for him.

In order to stop this madness, I believe we need to stop holding parents and children up to the impossible standards that society has placed on them. We need to realize that none of us will raise a perfect child, no matter how much we want to. Instead of looking for shortcuts in a pill or on a couch, we need to turn our attentions to educating society about what it means to be different, and more specifically what it means to be highly active in a world of people who aren't. This education needs to include the simple fact that highly active children have brains that function differently. That doesn't, of course, mean that these children are disordered or diseased; it simply means that they are different.

In his book *The Explosive Child,* Ross W. Greene points out that some of the most obvious differences in the brains of highly active children occur in their frontal lobe in what he refers to as their "executive functions." Executive functions are those skills that, among other things, include the ability to shift from one mind-set to another. Explaining to others that your child is not really spoiled, he just has a slight difference in his executive functions is impossible.

Besides, when it comes down to it, the truth is that most people simply don't care why a highly active child is the way he is. They just want the annoyance to stop. Richard Carlson writes about our intolerance in *Don't Sweat the Small Stuff*. He recounts the time when someone asked him to describe the average person in two words or less. His answer: "easily bothered." I can't think of a more accurate answer than that. Americans are easily bothered. We are bothered because we think in terms of convenience instead of gratitude. Instead of appreciating the stillness and divine intermission that occurs while we sit at a traffic light or wait in line at the bank, we chomp at the bit. Life has become a race instead of a journey for most adults. Unfortunately, this race is taking the greatest toll on our children. In general, all children, not just those who are different, have become an inconvenience.

Nevertheless, it's not too late to turn things around. It's not too late to start teaching tolerance to our children and to each other. As parents, though, we need to first experience a paradigm shift in our own beliefs about what it means to be a child, especially one who is naturally intense, active, and impulsive, before trying to educate society. For it is our outlook that needs altering, not our child's. Instead of resorting to psychoactive elixirs and ridiculously rigid rules of conduct, we have to trust our own instincts. We need to tune out advertising and tune in to our own hearts. I truly believe the key to helping our highly active children live up to their potential lies in what we perceive to be wrong in the first place.

As parents we need to reexamine our beliefs about what is acceptable behavior in our offspring and what is not. We need to remember that most children are annoying and loud and irritating. They spill things, get into trouble, throw tantrums, and are generally a pain in the neck. Thankfully, they do eventually grow up, but until then, we need to be more reasonable in our expectations of them.

We also need to be more reasonable in our expectations of ourselves. In addition to redefining what it means to be a child, we need to remember what it means to be a parent. Parenthood is a messy, annoying, and bothersome job. It means giving up sleep and vacations, and being embarrassed on plane trips and at restaurants. It also mean sacrificing, sacrificing, sacrificing. After all, it is a job that most of us volunteered for, and until someone comes up with a way to create perfect parents, the fact remains that there are not going to be any perfect children.

However, that doesn't mean that we need to relegate ourselves to seeing only the drudgery of parenthood. Raising children is a very rewarding and positive experience. It has its downside, but it most assuredly has its upside. And I believe that if we can keep our thoughts on what is so exceptionally right about our children, especially those who are highly active, then what's so wrong about them will eventually fade into the background.

8

What's Right About What's Wrong

"Activity. A-C-T-I-V-I-T-Y." Brandan prattles off the word with record speed. His lopsided grin reflects the obvious irony.

"Situat . . . ," I begin.

"S-I-T-U-A-T-I-O-N," he barks back before I have a chance to finish.

I continue calling out words to my son from the other side of the playroom. He answers with 100 percent accuracy. Most people would be amazed. Not just at his proficiency in spelling, but at the fact that while he is spelling he is also listening to a CD, jumping on a mini-trampoline, eating popcorn, and playing Nintendo. All at the same time. And all quite well.

Brandan's propensity for multitasking has been evident since he was an infant, when, in order to get him to nurse, I had to occupy both of his hands with toys and rock him at the same time. Even then it was a major effort to keep his tiny feet from rearing up and kicking me in the face.

I ignore the rock music screeching in the background and offer my game-playing, popcorn-eating kangaroo a challenge word, "expressive."

Brandan's eyes narrow as his brain cells shift into fourth gear. Short wisps of auburn hair fly straight up from his scalp with every rebound. He lets out a small grunt, tilts his head momentarily to the left, but literally doesn't miss a beat on the mini-trampoline or the word.

"E-X-P-R-E-S-S-I-V-E." His slender, shirtless torso springs into the air. He is nine, and I still can't seem to keep him fully dressed. Instead of battling with him over the issue of clothes, I have lowered the requirements of his attire to a minimum of underwear and shorts. Some days even the underwear is questionable. Today I feel lucky that he at least has his socks and shoes on.

I carefully contemplate the next word. I know that he, too, is anticipating my next linguistic serve. The sharp flickering movements of the video characters on the TV screen reflect in his eyes as I allow for an additional moment of suspense.

Just when he is about to protest my silence, I deliver. "Versatile!"

His disapproval is immediate. "Mom! That's not a spelling word!" Abandoning the controller momentarily, he snatches a handful of popcorn from the bookshelf to his right. He plops the majority of the white, fluffy kernels in his mouth without missing a beat. Scattered remains fall to the floor like snowflakes. "You've got to give me a real word."

"Versatile is a real word. It means being able to do more than one thing at a time," I say, folding up the piece of paper. "Like vacuuming up your mess, while putting on a shirt, while finishing the rest of your homework."

Brandan pretends not to understand the obvious hint and begins to sing along with the music.

I am feeling overwhelmed from all the stimulus and stand up to leave.

My half-naked, kaleidoscopic pogo stick of a son notices me leaving and immediately begins a verbal protest, all the while continuing his trampoline-maneuvering, Nintendo-playing, popcorn-eating performance. "Don't go, don't go," he begs. "I'll be s-o-o bored if you leave!"

I hesitate momentarily. I really would like to stay. Brandan is, after all, very entertaining to watch. However, my head is beginning to pound, and his aerodynamics are making me dizzy. Being with any nine-year-old boy for any length of time is draining. Being with Brandan on a continuous basis is enough to cause a nuclear melt-down. Opting for sanity, I ignore his pleas and head for the exit.

Still, I can't help but smile at my very versatile son, as I temporarily close the door between his world and mine. As hectic as it is living with Brandan, I know that my life would be incredibly lonely and incomplete without him in it.

Walking back down the hall, I hear his voice singing over the CD player. "Only shooting stars break the mo-o-l-ld!"

I HAVEN'T ALWAYS admired Brandan's nature. In fact, two years ago I would have screamed at him to turn off the music, warned him about the dangers of eating popcorn while jumping on the mini-trampoline, and admonished him for even thinking of playing a video game during homework time. After all, there are certain rules and codes of conduct to follow when dealing with schoolwork. Experts advocate finding a quiet, secluded space for children to study. At the very least, tradition dictates that they should also be stationary.

Because I am a mother and am automatically programmed to scan any given situation, determine what is wrong, and then fix it, I would have immediately put a stop to the sideshow. However, in doing this, I would have overlooked the amazing fact that Brandan can concentrate with such accuracy on so many things at once. I would have ignored his multitasking talents and highlighted his hyperkinetic conduct. And I would not have been alone in my judgments.

Human beings have a propensity for the negative. We tend to value obscurity and skepticism, always looking for the darkened cloud instead of the silver lining. I believe it is especially prevalent when we label a child as disordered. In the rush to find a remedy for the child's imperfections, we completely lose sight of his talents, gifts, and sheer creative genius. Which is a shame, because although spirited children are impulsive, inattentive, distractible, and downright annoying, they are also highly creative, independent, inventive, multitasking individuals. And when given the appropriate academic circumstances and encouragement, they also tend to be very bright. However because we choose to see only what is wrong, instead of what is so obviously right about them, the talents and gifts of these children are ignored.

This is especially true for children who have been labeled as hyperactive. We are so caught up with teaching them how to become responsible adults, that, in addition to medicating them and modifying them, we have completely overlooked what incredibly wonderful kids they are. We ignore the fact that they are voracious artists, musicians, inventors, and comedians. We forget how great they are at multitasking and selling their points. Instead we squash their independent and off-the-wall nature by force-feeding them antidotes that would turn them into focused, attentive, restrained adults. The irony is that by doing this, by trying to rid our highly active children of all the traits that we abhor, we are, in a way, pretty much throwing out our babies with the bathwater.

Many of those in the medical profession would say that this is not the objective of traditional interventions; that the goal of medication and zero tolerance is to rid the child of his negative traits without altering his positive ones. But I don't think this is possible with the case of highly active children. I don't believe we can sift the baby from the bathwater or separate the masterpiece from the scratched corners. The characteristics that we want to eradicate are often the ones that make the child so extraordinary in the first place.

I believe what we really need to do is learn how to integrate the shadows with the light, the bad with the good, and the negative behavior with the positive behavior. We must embrace all of our child's traits, not just the ones that we perceive to be of value. For all characteristics, both good and bad, form the essence of their divine nature. Without their impulsive behavior, there is no natural intuition. Without their daydreams, there is no imagination or creativity. And without their obstinacy there is no perseverance.

Debbie Ford does a wonderful job of expressing this concept in her book *The Dark Side of the Light Chasers.* In her groundbreaking work she writes, "We live under the impression that in order for something to be divine, it has to be perfect. We are mistaken. In fact, the opposite is true. To be divine is to be whole and to be whole is to be everything: the positive and the negative, the good and the bad, the holy man and the devil."

This belief, that to be divine means to express both positive and negative attributes, goes to the core of what we need to understand as parents and caregivers of highly active children. If we can grasp this concept and apply it to our view of our children, our perception of who they are will shift on its own. We will then intuitively celebrate our children's wholeness. We will automatically cherish those traits that we had previously fought so hard to eliminate. By integrating what's wrong with what's right, the natural light and unique divinity of the highly active child will eliminate any doubts we had about them.

In order to integrate his shadows with his light, though, a

spirited child needs to be supported by people who will help him redirect his energy, not squash it. He needs to have parents who are willing to help him steer his boat and integrate his shadows without demanding that he turn off the engine or the light. He also needs to be embraced by people who tell him that they love him without having to add the phrase "just the way you are" after it. Most important, he needs to be told that he is normal, even if the outside world doesn't always think so.

I realize that this may be difficult for many parents, especially those who were raised in more strict environments themselves, to resist the temptation to pick out their child's negative traits and fix them. It may be helpful for these parents to keep in mind that the goal is not to overlook the shadows, but to bring them into the light. The shadows, the negative traits, will not go away, but they can be put into the proper context so that parents, and society, can view the highly active child as the luminary that he truly is.

The easiest way to embrace a child's shadows is by suspending judgment and simply observing how the child functions on a daily basis. By observing how a child interacts with others, especially his peers, parents and caregivers can get an idea of how he uses his shadow traits to increase his stature with the outside world. For example, a child who is impulsive will naturally be the first to raise his hand in class. Unfortunately, he may also blurt out the answer before being called on. This is considered negative behavior in the classroom. But in a boardroom or sales meeting, jumping the gun may not be such a bad thing. In fact, it is the trait of movers and shakers.

In addition to viewing his gifts, being a neutral observer allows parents a unique opportunity to truly be able to identify with a hyperkinetic child. It also allows them to better understand what their spirited child feels, hears, sees, and smells. Parents can then take what they've learned about their child, and what it means to be highly active in a world that is not, and share it with others. An example that I always give when I am trying to explain what is going on in Brandan's brain is to ask the bystanders how they would feel if they had to drink ten cups of coffee and then sit through a boring lecture. There are many times when I am having a particularly bad day coping with my son that I must remind myself of my own explanation.

After parents or advocates have delegated themselves to being observers, they should list the qualities that they know to be true of their child. Although it is important to keep a positive feeling about the child, the exercise is not to avoid his negative traits or shadows, but to see them in the proper perspective. By describing the child in an impartial manner, the emotional aspect, which is what creates the drama that is attached to a hyperkinetic child, diminishes.

Over the past few years, I have become quite good at focusing my attention on Brandan's wholeness, allowing his bright light to naturally envelope his shadows. I have integrated his impulsive behavior with his spontaneous laughter, his inattention in with his ability to multitask, and his hyperkinetic activities in with his ambition. In order to truly free his spirit I have stopped highlighting what's wrong, and started celebrating what's right. This doesn't mean that I have donned a gigantic pair of rose-colored glasses. It simply means that I am able to take in the entire masterpiece that is my son all at once.

The first step in my own paradigm shift with Brandan came when I realized that I was going to have to change my vocabulary. Over the years I had become accustomed to negative labels to alleviate my own anxiety about his behavior. I threw around medical terms such as ADHD, and learned to speak the latest psychobabble in an effort to prove to all the bystanders that I was in control. I also openly exchanged horror stories about Brandan with other sympathetic parents. My downgraded vocabulary, in essence, became a safe haven for me, but it took its toll on my son. I could see that other people were beginning to peg him, too. One evening over dinner my friend Marianne Williamson pointed out to me that I had described Brandan as being hyperactive several times throughout the course of the meal. She then reminded me that by using the word "hyperactive," I was tagging him as a child who was disordered. She was right. The word *hyperactive* in itself denotes a disease, as does *attention deficit disorder*. Since that evening I have been careful not to use either of those terms in describing my son. Instead, I choose words that more accurately described his wholeness and his strengths.

Brandan is no longer obstinate, he is tenacious. He is no longer impulsive; he is instinctive. He is not hyperactive; he is highly active. He is not distractible; he is highly aware. He is not impatient; he is excitable. He is not a daydreamer; he is imaginative. He is not oppositional; he is self-assured. Most important, he is not disordered; he is gifted. Since I began using my new vocabulary, I have not only seen a positive change in Brandan, but I have noticed that others have started to react more openly to him as well.

In addition to changing my vocabulary, I have also come up with a list of Brandan's shadow traits that I have integrated into his light. The most obvious characteristic on my list is Brandan's hyperawareness—his intense, amplified comprehension of life. It is this one trait, this exaggerated awareness of all things true, which complicates and frustrates the lives of most highly active children. It is the gift that becomes the albatross around their souls when they cannot explain their unique perceptions to the world. It is from this one trait that a whole list of secondary features arise.

These secondary shadow features can best be classified as the coping skills that have arisen as a result of the child's hyperawareness of his surroundings. Because these shadows are not inherent, but individual reactions, they vary from child to child. As with all coping skills, they tend to expand in response to our ever-complicated society. Hence, the increase in "symptoms" being attributed to highly active children. These traits include: hyperkinetic behavior, distractibility, impulsivity, inflexibility, impatience, selfishness, daydreaming, aggression, and conduct disorders.

Hyperkinetic, or highly active, energy is perhaps one of the most obvious secondary traits, and it is also one of the most annoying. Fortunately, it is also one of the easiest shadows to integrate. Even the most rigid of parents can foresee how this abundance of energy will eventually work to a child's advantage. After all, who wouldn't want to have that much energy to finish the day's activities? One of the best ways to integrate this shadow is to acknowledge how truly difficult it is for a spirited child to stay in the same spot for more than two seconds. Emotionally, physically, and spiritually, these children cannot sit still. They are in divine motion. They are on this earth to accomplish twice as much as the rest of us. As they grow, they will be able to streamline their excessive energy. Until then, arrangements need to be made to either direct their energy, or refrain from putting the child in a situation where he or she will have to remain stationary for long periods at a time. I no longer request that Brandan sit through an adult church service or any other lecture over thirty minutes. I also avoid extended trips in the car and lengthy plane rides. Although some experts would disagree, I simply don't feel that forcing a highly active child to remain motionless is in anyone's best interest.

Another secondary trait that directly ties in with a child's hyperawareness is distractibility. Because spirited children have the ability to focus on and pay attention to so many events at once, they sometimes miss the minor details. This brings about labels of being inattentive or a daydreamer, which cannot be further from the truth. By their very nature, highly active children are very attentive. It's just that they are not always paying attention to what we want them to.

Brandan can scan and scrutinize every molecule in his world. And miraculously he can do it all at once. I used to think that my son was zoning out; now I see that he is really zoning in. At school he is aware of the butterfly outside the window, his seatmate's sneeze, the children walking in the hallway, as well as the teacher talking in front of the class. Unfortunately, this hyperawareness of every event often causes a problem, because while Brandan is studying the butterfly on the window ledge, he is missing what the teacher is saying.

In order to maximize this trait, parents and teachers need to be aware that the child is not ignoring them on purpose. He is just trying to sort through all the stimulus he is receiving. Standing close to a highly active child, or touching his shoulder, usually remedies this problem by bringing the child's attention back to the desired spot.

The third most common trait, impulsiveness, is perhaps one of the hardest for parents to appreciate and integrate. Over the years impulsivity has come to be quite a derogatory term. It is often used to describe someone who has absolutely no control over their actions. But this is simply not true. By definition, impulsive means the act of driving onward. And that is what the highly active child does. Brandan's spirit moves quickly, not out of whim, but out of inspiration. Because he is curious by nature, he inevitably seeks to know the unknown and to attain the unattainable, and he seeks it with every cell in his body.

Unfortunately, this type of intense motion causes children like Brandan to crash head-on into whatever it is they are seeking to understand. Boredom can compound the problem, and pretty soon their impetuous nature is leading them directly down the down the rocky road of risk taking and thrill seeking. Many parents then try to eradicate any type of whimsical behavior because they see it as a physical hazard.

The truth is that being impulsive can be dangerous, especially for teenagers learning to drive. It can be equally as hazardous when riding a bike, playing near the street, or even in one's own room.

Nevertheless, having an impulsive nature does have its advantages. Impulsive people are those who are able to think on their feet in any given situation and are great at making last-minute improvisations. They are also the self-starters of the world who don't need outside prompters to get a project going. Furthermore, in learning to accept a child's impulsive nature, parents have to remember that life is a gamble. Whether it means walking down the street or walking down the stairs, accidents and incidents abound in the world. There is no getting around the fact that our days are filled with risks. Without these risks, life is not only monotonous, but it is joyless. In weighing the negative consequences and dangers of Brandan's impulsive behavior with this fact, I have learned to loosen his reins a little more with each passing day.

Being irritable, which is another common characteristic of spirited children, is not only uncomfortable for the children who are experiencing it, but is also difficult for everyone who must be around them. Being in the general vicinity of a child who is not only hyperkinetic and impulsive, but cranky at the same time, is usually more than parents can take. However, being irritable is a natural reaction to living in a world where everything and everyone is taken in through the senses.

The ability to shut out unwanted information is something that most people take for granted. They have no idea how annoying it can be. To get a clearer picture of what highly active children go through, one can imagine being locked in a room twenty-four hours a day with the radio blasting at full volume. A person's nerves would be shot. They would be irritable, oppositional, defiant, moody, and all the adjectives that are used to describe the accelerated spirit. When one's brain is constantly being bombarded with various stimuli, there is no peace. The body's internal engines are revved up. Any attempt to shut them down only compounds the problem.

I have found the best way to integrate this shadow trait in Brandan is to make a joke out of it. Bringing humor into any given situation often has a way of shedding light on it. There are many days, though, when I know that nothing I do will change the fact that he is going to be grumpy and irritable. On these days I abandon any attempt at pacifying him and concentrate on my own needs, knowing that, like all of us, working through a bad mood is often something that is best done alone.

A whole host of other shadow traits come as a result of the shame and discouragement that highly active children experience through negative interactions. Although these characteristics, such as anxiety, sadness, compulsive behavior, and sleeplessness, may be a result of a chemical imbalance, more often then not they are simply responses that the child is putting out to alert his parents and caregivers that something is terribly wrong with his environment. As with Brandan, these features can be exacerbated by medicines that are prescribed by well-meaning physicians. Or they can be intensified by being in an overwhelming school situation. Therefore, before attempting to integrate these shadow traits into a child, it is important to first make sure that these characteristics are truly a part of the child's personality, and not a sign that the child's environment needs to be reexamined. The best way to discern if something in a child's environment is causing his sad moods is to ask and to keep asking. It is also important to keep listening. More often than not children themselves are the best indicators of what is wrong. If parents are still not able to tell if the problem is external or internal and the child is entering a prolonged period (two or more weeks) of severe depression or sad moods, then it is extremely important that he or she be seen by a physician for further evaluation.

In addition to changing my semantics about Brandan and learning to integrate his positive characteristics with his negative ones, I have also come up with a working definition that I believe accurately describes him. This definition not only reminds me that my son, though not perfect, is still a very talented and resourceful person, but it also reminds the world.

The working definition I have of Brandan goes something like this: "My child is intense, creative, and driven. He has a hard time coping with new situations and sometimes acts out his frustrations in inappropriate ways. He is very giving and loving to animals and other children. He is a people person and loves participating in activities and being a part of the group. He is sometimes loud and opinionated, and it is sometimes necessary for adults around him to redirect his strong energy level when he steps over the line. He is good in math and sports and has difficulty with small motor skills such as hand-writing. He moves at a fast pace and it is hard to get him to slow down once he gets going."

It is important to avoid using the words *but, also, however,* and *although* when defining a spirited child. It is also better to give the facts in a neutral tone. State the way the child is. No excuses, no apologies, no explanations, and no labels. If someone comments on my child's behavior, or if they outright ask if he is hyperactive, I smile and say, "Brandan is intense and creative." That simple statement takes the stigma and the unwanted sympathy out of the label.

Once a parent has a good working definition of what they know to be true about their child, they can begin sharing it with others. This helps grandparents, teachers, neighbors, and friends see what's so wonderfully right about the highly active child. A good working definition may fall on deaf ears at first if parents are discussing their child with longtime friends and family members. But as time goes on, if parents keeps reiterating their new definition of their child, others will begin to see him or her in a different light, too.

Children, themselves, also need to be taught what is incredibly right about them. Highly active children receive negative feedback from bystanders on a continuous basis and this often causes a problem with their self-esteem. Parents and caregivers must step in and show them how to integrate their own shadows with their light. Spirited children need to be told that each and every trait they posses is a gift. For a child's desire to feel good about himself, even when he senses that he is different, is the key to his leading a happy, successful life.

Only after I began to see what was so right about what seemed wrong with Brandan did I truly understand that freeing his spirit was not just about letting him be who he was, it was about loving who he was. Yet, I also knew freeing his spirit required teaching him ways to harmonize his energy with the outside world. For it is not enough to simply cut the ropes and turn a child into the wind. In order to be truly free a child must be able to function in society. He must eventually learn to blend his energy with those who dance to a slower tune if he is to have happy, healthy, successful relationships. With this in mind, I began to focus my attentions on how I could direct Brandan's energy in a positive way without putting the brakes on his divine spirited nature.

9

Directing the Energy of a
Highly Active Child

It is 5:33 P.M. and I am scurrying through the house in search of my nine-year-old son's right shoe. Brandan is notorious for losing his footwear. A matching pair never ends up in the same spot. When he was young, I used to tie the laces of each shoe together to avoid this last minute maneuvering. Now that he is nine, I refuse to do that, and make him hunt for them himself or wear a mismatched pair. I have agreed to help him out today, only because he has spent the afternoon doing homework.

I survey the living room one last time and am just about to give up when I see the black tip of the displaced cleat peeking out from under the plant in the foyer. I retrieve the shoe and scream for Brandan to hurry.

Brandan appears at the top of the staircase in his padded white pants and socks. He is carrying one cleat, one helmet, one mouth guard, one set of shoulder pads, a football, and his practice jersey. He smiles when he sees I have found the missing shoe and gallops down the steps to greet me. I take the equipment from him and head for the minivan while he retrieves his water bottle from the refrigerator.

At 5:36 I start the engine, and we are off. Halfway down the block I think to ask Brandan about his protective cup. He pretends not to hear me at first, and when I repeat the question, he remarks on how late we are. I glance at the clock on the dashboard. We are indeed already six minutes behind schedule. However, my husband rightfully insists that Brandan wear this particular piece of equipment during all games and practices, and although I am no expert in how it feels to be hit in the groin without one, I am told it is not pleasant. I immediately back up the van.

Brandan protests again, but I am firm. In the house he goes. Off go the cleats and the pants; on goes the protective cup. Brandan is redressed and back in the van in under four minutes. Once more we are maneuvering through the neighborhood at breakneck speed. Football practice starts promptly at 6 P.M. and our house is a thirty-minute drive from the practice field. The pressure to be on time to kids' athletic events is undeniably ridiculous, and I am embarrassed to be included in the millions of men and women who drive erratically in the name of their child's sport. However, Brandan's coach is the Mike Ditka of youth football, and if a player arrives even one minute late to practice he is forced to do "six inches"—an exercise that sounds harmless enough, but according to my son falls under the punishment known as "the ring of pain." Therefore I forgo the holier-than-thou attitude about soccer moms and lean on the gas pedal.

Brandan puts on his cleats and the rest of his equipment while I drive. As we near the freeway, I am horrified to see that it is a virtual parking lot. I decide to take an alternate route, which I hope will be quicker. However, this shortcut entails maneuvering several major intersections. Our aging red minivan weaves in and out of traffic like a fire engine on the way to a blaze. We make all of the green lights except the last. Brandan momentarily looks up as we come to a grinding halt, glances around at the unfamiliar surroundings, and asks, "Are we lost again?" His voices sounds nervous and tense and I know that he is worried about the "six inches."

I assure him that we are not lost and am grateful that my instinct to take a different route is correct when we arrive at the playing field two minutes early.

"Come watch me," Brandan pleads as he scrambles across the seat. Since my husband is usually in charge of sports activities, I rarely get to see my son play, except at games. I put aside the book that I had brought to read, and retrieve my lawn chair from the trunk.

Brandan is immediately greeted with a hard pop on his helmet from Coach Ditka. I wince slightly, but know that it is the universal sign of affection among football players. I also know that Brandan's head is well protected in the padded plastic bubble. He swaggers over to his place in line with the other boys. It is odd how he instantly becomes a new child the minute he is in full football regalia. His shoulders are pushed back, and his entire body moves with an air of importance. The other players greet Brandan with high fives as he falls into place.

I find a spot on the sideline with the other parents and settle into my chair.

The whistle blows and the players begin their jumping jacks. With the exception of one or two boys, they clamor along in sync, screaming out the count. After they have pushed and pulled and strained and stretched every muscle, they begin their drills. The boys are divided into two groups, offense and defense. Brandan is on defense tonight. For the next two hours I watch on the lighted football field as Ditka directs Brandan's excessive energy through body slams, timed races, and laps around the field. From where I am sitting, my son does not look any wilder than the other boys. They all tend to bounce off of each other like testosterone-driven pinballs.

At the end of practice, the boys huddle together to chant their mantra "good, better, best, never let it rest, until the good is better and the better best." They then proceed to make growling noises and other deep-throated sounds at each other, flexing their muscles like miniature bodybuilders. Ditka finishes the session with a quick pep talk on the upcoming game.

On the way home, Brandan's body is exhausted but his brain is still in high gear. He rattles on about his performance, questioning me relentlessly about each of the plays to see if I was paying attention. I assure him that I saw each and every tackle, maneuver, and body slam. I praise him on his flexibility and speed. I mention the sack he made during the scrimmage. Together, we review every moment of the two-hour practice.

At home, Brandan gives another play-by-play review to his father and sister before heading to the shower. Within two minutes of brushing his teeth and getting into his pajamas, he is fast asleep on the couch.

ONE OF THE most difficult tasks of raising a spirited child is knowing what to do with their excess energy. The power and strength of a highly active child, like the atomic bomb, is staggering. It can quickly go from productive to destructive in a matter of seconds.

Many professionals claim that the best way to handle this excess energy is through structure. The truth is that they are right. Highly active children do need structure. Unfortunately, too many of these same professionals inadvertently equate structure with restraint. Another truth is that consistently repressing a child's energy has the unexpected effect of backfiring.

Imposing stringent rules on a child who is intense and strong willed only forces the child to be resentful and combative. Authoritative parenting may also cause the child's already intense feelings to manifest as rage. This in turn results in the child being labeled as out of control. However, nothing can be further from the truth.

In fact, one of the biggest misconceptions about highly active children is that they are always ill-tempered. I have read countless books over the years that have listed rage as a trait of an ADHD child. It's as if professionals believe that these children are born foaming at the mouth. The truth is that while highly active children do tend to reach a boiling point faster than the average child, they are no more genetically predisposed to flying off into a violent rage than anyone else. Highly active children may display anger and other emotions on a greater frequency than the average child, but it is usually out of frustration. Most of these children live in a world where their excessive energies and emotions are consistently being thwarted, obstructed, and bottled up by everyone around them. It is no wonder that they are labeled as hotheads.

Instead of restraints, I believe what these gifted, intense, and passionate children need is appropriate channels for their energy. Again, the goal is to free their spirits, not control them. Putting a lid on a child who is already boiling out of the pot is not the answer. Highly active children need physical and mental releases that will allow them to direct their energy in a positive, constructive manner, not cemented walls. These children also need options, and lots of them. By providing them with choices as well as direction, they often excel physically, mentally, and emotionally, as well as spiritually.

That doesn't mean, of course, that parents should completely turn over the reins to their children. Highly active children need a fair amount of direction and assistance in using their energy in a positive way. Like all their gifts, their excess energy has two directions in which to travel—a positive, externalizing, constructive road, or a negative, internalizing, destructive one. The positive, externalizing use of energy is what these children use to create miracles that not only illuminate their lives, but brighten the lives of those around them. The destructive internalizing use of excess energy is what makes them appear self-centered and unfeeling. It can also bring about bouts of depression, anxiety, and anger.

Keeping a child's energy flowing in a positive, externalized way is not easy, though. The trick comes in pointing the child in the right direction without retarding his resolve. I have found the most effective way to keep Brandan's energy focused and on track is to enroll him in activities that combine a physical challenge with a mental one.

Organized sports are perhaps the best way to streamline a child's intense nature, both mentally and physically. Never is Brandan's confidence level as high as it is when he is with his teammates. Nor is his energy as concentrated or as focused as it is after a practice or a game. In retrospect, I am convinced that organized sports were one of the biggest keys to unlocking the cage that encased Brandan's soul. But I didn't always hold that perspective. In fact, there were many times when I questioned his involvement in athletics all together.

When my husband first enrolled Brandan in soccer at the age of five, I was certain that his attention span was too short to focus on the game. Yet the coaches and other players didn't seem to mind that he daydreamed. When he was six and wanted to play baseball, I was convinced that he would never be able to play a position without wandering off the field. Yet, the coaches and my husband worked with him until he learned to play first base quite well. When he asked to play football at eight, I would have bet the house that he was going to quit before the season was over. The workouts were tough, the discipline was strict. Once again, he proved me wrong.

Two years ago, at nine, when Brandan asked to play basketball, I again protested. Basketball is an indoor sport, and while he does quite well in the open air, I was positive that being in an enclosed gym with the distracting noise of the spectators would be too much. As it turns out, basketball is not only his favorite sport, but it's the one he is most talented at playing.

Over the years there have been times when Brandan was impatient and inattentive, but the majority of his coaches have been understanding and supportive. They have worked tirelessly and effortlessly to help him direct his excess energy. In fact, these coaches have nurtured Brandan's spirit in a way that no therapist or physician could have. They have made him stronger physically and emotionally, and they have also helped him to see himself not as a wild and out-of-control boy, but as a talented young athlete.

Through competitive sports, Brandan has earned respect from his peers, and he has gained acceptance and admiration from the spectators. On the field he is gifted and talented, not disordered. On the court he is swift and agile, not hyper. His excess energy is not only given an outlet, it is given a spotlight.

I believe that encouraging highly active children to participate in sports is imperative to freeing their spirits. Being involved in sports allows them the opportunity to showcase their energy. It also takes their born-to-be-wild nature and streamlines it into a valuable resource. Once a child views his excessive energy as an asset rather than an obstruction, he becomes motivated to seek out other avenues in which to make a positive impact.

Furthermore, when parents fortify their child's energy through sports, instead of strangling it through medicine and other ropes, they are helping them carve out a place for themselves in the world. For a child truly cannot succeed in life if he cannot grasp his own self-worth and genuine nature. It is up to parents to help their child see his unique and rare gifts. And it is up to parents to teach their child how to take his obstructions and turn them into bridges, and how to take his disadvantages and turn them into opportunities.

Unfortunately, children's sports have received a bad name over the past few years because parents have a hard time keeping their own emotions in line. Nearly all organizations that involve children claim that they concentrate on skill and fun rather than winning or losing; however, this is not always the case. Different leagues have different philosophies on the best way to coach children. Some leagues are quite competitive, while others are more relaxed. Therefore it is imperative that parents check out the league or circuit before they enroll their child to find out its overall philosophy. They may also want to speak with other parents whose children participate in the league.

It is also important to speak with the child's coach before the season begins to find out his or her individual philosophy. Although rarely will one bad season or coach deter a child from wanting to participate in sports again, too many disappointments or discouraging seasons can damage a child's self-esteem and backfire on a parent's effort to streamline their child's energy in a constructive manner. Therefore, coaches, like teachers, need to be informed about the energetic nature of the highly active child and how to best direct it.

Keeping a highly active child involved in sports isn't the only direction to take. For children who are not athletic, or who show little interest in sports, there are many other avenues that taper a child's energy without crushing their spirit.

One way is to channel the child's energy and intense emotions into a Herculean feat. Brandan received a pogo stick for his ninth birthday and spent the entire summer trying to break the Guinness World Record for the number of consecutive jumps. Of course, shattering the record was entirely beyond his ability, but that didn't stop him from at least trying. He became the most prolific pogo stick bouncer our neighborhood has ever seen. Not only did he learn balance and mobility, but his pogo-popping performance kept him from getting into mischief the entire summer.

The most important thing to remember when guiding a child's energy is that the rate at which a child's spirit flows is not nearly as important as the direction it flows. Parents and caregivers must find activities that keep a child's energy from becoming scattered as well as keep his spirit intact. One activity Brandan picked up from his Uncle Karl was yoga. Yoga may seem like a rather simple, mindless activity. But mastering the various yoga positions takes an enormous amount of mental and physical concentration. This intense focus stimulates the brain as well as the body and can streamline a spirited child's energy in amazing ways.

Art and drawing is another activity that can heighten a child's attention span. Although art doesn't require a lot of physical movement, it can be a great outlet. Often the concentration that it takes to create a piece of art is enough to release the intense emotions that the child is feeling. Many parents claim that art is also the best emotional outlet because it doesn't tend to rev up a child's engine the way sports does. Plus, there are many highly active children who simply don't enjoy competitive sports. They find that they would rather work alone, or side by side with their peers instead of interfacing with them. Like sports, art comes in many different forms; one to match each child's personality and skills.

Although it is best to undertake an activity that utilizes a child's physical and mental abilities at the same time, employing a mental exercise by itself is also helpful. For intellectual stimulation, Brandan enjoys saying the alphabet backward and working puzzles and math problems. Other mental challenges include learning a new language, or making up a language or secret code.

Hobbies are yet another great way for a parent to streamline a child's energy. At one time Brandan's favorite hobby was magic. Conjuring up magic has always been intriguing to children; it gives them a sense of power over their environment, as well as teaching them a new skill. Another fun hobby is collecting. Highly active children are pack rats by nature, and the art of collecting is a perfect way to put that skill to use. Although coin and stamp collecting are perhaps two of the most obvious choices, collecting can include almost anything a child is interested in. Other hobbies include assembling airplanes or model cars. Once, I heard a father say that he has an old lawn mower in the back that he let his spirited son take apart and put back together as a way to streamline his excess energy.

Although most parents try to discourage their highly active child from participating in anything that requires too much supervision, the use of science projects, chemistry, and wood-burning sets is an excellent way to channel a child's energy into a profession. One of the most profound gifts of highly active children is their intense curiosity. They like to tinker and explore and learn how things work. This heightened curiosity is one of the reasons they seem to get into so much trouble all the time. Nevertheless, if their curiosity is satisfied and expanded through the use of science, parents may find their highly active dynamo turning his challenge into a truly rewarding career.

On the other hand, if a spirited child's energy is not directed in a positive manner, parents will find themselves caught in some ferocious battles. Left to their own devices, highly active children will create their own entertainment. At the very least this involves mischief. At its worst, undirected energy over a long period of time coupled with an already frustrated child can quickly turn into rage and violence. In fact, parents who neglect to teach their highly active child how to streamline his energy early on may find themselves caught in hand-to-hand combat as he or she enters the turbulent tide of the teenage years. Life then can become miserable for all concerned as parents fight to stay on their feet and out of their child's wake.

10

Choosing Battles and Staying Out of the Wake

The slamming door along with the sound of my nine-year-old son's backpack crashing to the floor interrupts my work.

"Mom!" screams Brandan. From the tone of his voice I can tell exactly what type of day he had at school. The forecast doesn't look good. My neck muscles tighten as I brace myself for the approaching storm.

"Mom!" The echo is getting closer. In an attempt to secure a few more minutes of work, I remain silent. However, Brandan eventually ferrets me out of my hiding spot in the kitchen and descends upon me like a dark cloud.

He throws all ninety pounds of himself on my lap. Although he is clearly in emotional pain, I risk the rhetorical question, "How was school today?" It is a script that we play out once a week, Brandan and I. Me pretending not to notice that he is horrifically upset, and him dramatically acting out his pain without saying a word. He inhales deeply, and then releases a long-winded sigh that literally sounds as though it ought to be accompanied by violins. He waits for me to ask again, and when I withhold my prompting, he squirms on my lap. His purpose, of course, is to make me as physically uncomfortable as he is emotion-ally—and it works. My thighs and knees cannot take the weight and begin to buckle under the pressure.

I attempt to brush him off. "You're too big. Get out of my lap."

Brandan reluctantly complies. But once on his feet, his arms lock around my neck in a death grip.

"Sit down over there, and TELL me what happened at school today," I gasp, prying his arms from around my neck.

Brandan hurls himself into the nearest chair and be-gins to unload the dreadful details of his disastrous day. "I was late for school and I'm not going to be able to go to recess if I'm late again this week," he begins. He takes another deep breath for theatrical effect, and then contin-ues. "I didn't get to sit with my friends at lunch because all the chairs were taken. And, I got a hole in my jeans at recess."

I look down at his pants. They not only have a hole, they are split from the knee to the ankle. It is obvious that the rip is no accident. However, I withhold my accusations until Brandan has finished commiserating.

"And also . . ." he fumbles to find something else to add to his rather short list of overstated tribulations. "My stomach hurts!" He again dramatizes his disposition by doubling over in the chair, his arms clutching his midsection as though he has just been shot.

I learned a long time ago that playing along with Brandan's histrionics is the quickest and easiest way to get him out of his mood, so I muster as much distress as I possibly can. "Oh, that's awful. I can't believe that all happened in one day."

Continuing to spin my web of motherly comfort, I encourage Brandan to give details about the events. "I bet you were terribly humiliated when you found out you were late."

Brandan immediately perks up when he sees how concerned I am. "Uh-huh," he says, sitting straight up in the chair. "Everyone was looking at me."

"And why didn't you get to sit with your friends at lunch? Didn't they save you a place?"

"No!" Brandan moans, feeling every bit of his self-righteous indignation.

I gasp and wait for him to continue. But by this time, he is growing bored with his act, and is now rummaging through the pantry. I decide this is as good a time as any to ask him about the ripped jeans. "And how did your pants get torn?"

Brandan glances down at his jeans, and a slight smile crosses his face. "Well, actually, I had a hole in them and I messed with it until it ripped."

His gut-wrenching stomachache has mysteriously disappeared, and he begins to boil water for his ramen noodles. I see that my role as Florence Nightingale is finished and return to my work at the kitchen table.

Brandan's mood is not over just yet. By the time his older sister has arrived home from school, his surly attitude is back in full force. He kicks off his persecution by purposely sitting on her legs while she is on the couch.

Unfortunately, Amanda is not quite as solicitous with him as I am. "Get off, now!"

Brandan responds to her demand by squirming even harder. Amanda retaliates by shoving him to the floor face first. Within minutes a full-blown brawl is underway in the middle of the living room. In order to save my glass-top coffee table and my sanity, I stop my work and separate them. Brandan immediately begins to laminate the situation. "I don't feel well and she won't let me sit on the couch."

I tell Brandan that he needs to go to bed if he is sick. However, my advice is lost in a whirlwind of other complaints. He can't find his homework. The tire on his bike is flat. There is no one to play with. He's hungry, but there's nothing in the pantry that he wants to eat. Like a caged lion, he roams up and down the stairs and from room to room, adding to his list of grievances as he goes.

I can see that the storm is picking up speed, and I debate about whether or not I should allow the intensity to build, or attempt to diffuse it before it turns into a full-fledged hurricane. There are many days when I don't have a choice. On these days I am forced to ride the wake of the storm, tied to Brandan's speeding boat, until the hurricane blows over and he eventually falls asleep, or until the pressure is released through a major explosion. From the way things are escalating, I know this is one of those days when I am going to have to batten down the hatches early. We are in for quite a storm.

By dinnertime, the gale is approaching land. My husband exacerbates Brandan's foul mood by engaging the energy. "Tomorrow after school I want you to clean the garage before you go out and play."

Brandan uses his utensil like a pitchfork, stabbing his salad with the intensity of a farmer baling hay. "I can't. I have homework."

"You don't know if you have homework yet," my husband admonishes.

"Yes, I do. I have to study my spelling words."

"Study them tonight."

"I can't. I have to watch wrestling."

Amanda and I snicker, but my husband will not be sidetracked. He is the only person I know who can out-rival Brandan's determination to get what he wants.

"You don't have to watch wrestling. As a matter of fact, I forbid you to watch TV until the garage is cleaned up and your homework is done."

The wind speed of the emotional storm goes from 50 to 200 m.p.h. in a matter of seconds as Hurricane Brandan blasts in full force. Slamming down his fork, he jumps up from the table. "Why can't I just clean it up on Saturday?"

Oblivious to the turbulent weather, my husband continues to eat.

Brandan repeats his overture, his voice rising until it breaks.

My husband delivers his pat answer, "because I said so," without even looking up. His calming presence in the middle of what is obviously only the beginning of Brandan's full-blown tantrum is amazing. I get nervous just listening to my son's piercing tone. Amanda, too, is sensing the foul weather and scoots her chair away from her brother.

"You never let me do anything," Brandan screams. He stomps out of the room, circles the staircase, and is back within seconds. "Why can't you just leave me alone?"

My husband is unaffected. He continues to eat as though there were nothing but elevator music playing in the background. Amanda and I finish dinner and seek shelter in her room. Even on the other side of the house, Brandan can be heard ranting and raving. I am sure that the neighbors hear the screaming, too. From the shrillness of his voice, I am sure that they think we are torturing him, and are at this very moment debating whether or not to call the police.

Eventually, the whirlwind winds down. Brandan stomps off to his room, slamming the door behind him. Five minutes later he is back in the kitchen, acting as if nothing has happened. Another major storm has passed.

Sensing that it is safe, Amanda and I come out of the bedroom. Passing by her brother, Amanda comments, "You have an anger management problem."

Brandan stops for a minute. A puzzled look crosses his

face. "No, I don't. I just have a lot more feelings inside to get out."

THIS IS PROBABLY one of the most profound statements that has ever come out of Brandan's mouth. For highly active children do tend to have a lot more feelings to get out. Unfortunately, these overflows of emotions, which include love, hate, anger, and grief, take center stage in their lives, causing them, and everyone around them, to feel as if they are on a never-ending roller coaster of highs and lows.

To sum it up in one word, highly active children are intense. And their fervor isn't just emotional. They are also mentally, spiritually, and physically very passionate people. It is why they are tactile learners. It is why they tend to have sensory issues. It is why they are so spiritual. And most visibly, it is why they have a hard time containing their feelings.

What complicates matters even more is that these intense emotions frequently tend to fluctuate. Brandan's poignant feelings can mean that one minute I'll get a bear hug so tight that I can't breathe, and the next minute I'll be standing in the middle of a full-blown gale. In looking up the word intense, I was not the least bit surprised to find both "brilliance" and "darkness" listed under its heading. Brandan is both brilliant and dark, occasionally at the same time. Sometimes I wonder if he isn't brilliant because he is dark. Or maybe it is just that his darkness originates from his brilliance. Whatever the case, living with him is not always easy.

In fact, it can be downright nerve-racking. Though highly active children rarely cause serious harm, their extreme emotions can frighten even the most experienced moms and dads. This emotional turmoil can be especially hard on stoic parents who take pride in their ability to control their own emotions, or for those who believe that boys shouldn't express their feelings. It can also be difficult on authoritative parents who believe that their child's outbursts are somehow a reflection on their own parenting skills.

Over the years I have learned not to take Brandan's ranting personally. Although my husband has always been more adept at ignoring the emotional eruptions than I have, I, too, am slowly learning to tune them out. I have come to understand that Brandan is not overreacting as a way to misbehave. He is simply having a hard time containing what he feels.

I have also come to understand that Brandan uses his strong emotions as a way of connecting to those around him. It is a way in which he can moor his speeding boat with solid ground. Granted, screaming at the top of his lungs may not be the best avenue for accomplishing this task, but for immature and highly active children, it is sometimes the only way they know. Parents who understand that their child is trying to forge a bond, and in turn, reach out to the child rather than push him or her away, find their child's emotions are much easier to manage as he or she matures.

One of the best ways I have found to handle Brandan's storms is to eliminate all my predetermined ideas about how he should express himself. I have also tried to rid my mind of any type of labels that may influence my actions toward him.

Once I see that a meltdown is inevitable, I immediately shift my own feelings into a lower gear, and attempt to distance myself from the impending explosion. This doesn't mean I disconnect from Brandan. Knowing that his intention is to connect with me through his emotions, I want him to feel as if he is being heard. I want him to know that I am there for him. I just don't want to engage the energy to the point that I am screaming back at him.

In essence, my objective is to stay connected to Brandan, but disconnected from the situation. This can best be accomplished by conversely extracting the root of the problem. For example, I start by attempting to put into words what Brandan can't or isn't saying. If I think he is feeling left out, I immediately acknowledge how hard it is to be excluded. This lets him know that not only am I aware that his feelings are hurt, but that I am concerned about them. I continue to sympathize with him until he is either bored with me or is distracted by something else. I also attempt to get him to explain in detail what it is that he is feeling.

However, I do draw the line at Brandan's commiserating the minute it looks as though it might turn violent. I am all for allowing him to vent his feelings, as long as his self-expression doesn't become destructive. I don't only mean physical destructiveness. Threatening, swearing, and other forms of verbal abuse are simply not tolerated in our house. I believe that all children, even highly active ones, need to know that being upset isn't an excuse for hurting others.

Occasionally Brandan's storms do threaten to cross the line, although he knows the consequences. For times like these, I have attempted to show him various ways in which he can discharge the pressure before he becomes destructive. The first and probably easiest way is by simply allowing him a quick release from the pressure. Dr. Michael Gurian, author of *The Wonder of Boys,* often speaks about the male propensity for "quick release." He states that while females tend to release their anger slowly over a period of time, males tend to want to release their anger quickly. After this release they are better able to cope. I have found this especially true of Brandan. Most of the time, if I allow him to get his anger out all at once, by hitting a pillow or a punching bag, he is able to put his animosity behind him fairly quickly.

Another coping skill that I have taught Brandan is that of the release valve. I have explained to him that by acknowledging and working out his frustration every time it occurs, it is less likely to build into a major explosion. As an example, I took out a balloon and blew it up, showing him, that if the air is released slowly, a little bit at a time, the balloon never gets so big that it pops.

However, despite my efforts to diffuse Brandan's emotions, or to have Brandan diffuse them himself, there are many days when nothing I do helps. In fact, I have found that sometimes trying to get him to work out his feelings only makes matters worse. These are the days when Brandan simply has to own up to the consequences that go along with losing his temper.

At times like these, I have found that the greatest natural teacher is that of cause and effect. Cause and effect, also known as "what goes around comes around" and more popularly as "natural consequence," means that for every action taken, there is a certain reaction. It is an inescapable, universal law that even the cleverest highly active child cannot maneuver out of. Like taxes and death, cause and effect is one of the great truths of life that no one is immune to.

Cause and effect is one of the best tools in teaching children because it takes the power out of the parent's hands and puts it in the hands of the universe, a power that cannot be cajoled, reckoned with, or bribed. It keeps parents out of the wake and away from the battle. And most important, it forces a child to be completely accountable for his behavior.

Sometimes, though, natural consequences aren't apparent, and the parent simply has to put a stop to the overflow of emotions that are streaming from their child. I call this engaging the energy, and although my husband tends to use it more liberally with Brandan, I try to save it as a last resort. Engaging the energy means going toe to toe with the child. It means battling it out to the bitter end. When children are younger, this is pretty easy. But once a child has entered puberty and the teenage years, the war zone can get pretty fierce, and knowing when to choose a battle is half the battle itself.

A great way to determine what to go to battle over is found in *The Explosive Child* by Ross W. Greene. In his book, Dr. Greene suggests that parents make three lists. The first list should contain behaviors they absolutely will not tolerate under any circumstances. The second list should consist of behaviors they will tolerate—even though they are annoying. And the third list is behaviors they are willing to negotiate.

Dr. Greene recommends that parents put safety in the first list of behaviors that will not be tolerated, and all other behaviors be divided up into the other two lists. However, I believe that there are other behaviors that parents should not have to tolerate besides safety issues. Therefore, I have added a number of other things to the first list. One of the things I absolutely will not tolerate is disrespect. And I don't mean just disrespect of adults. I mean disrespect for all of God's creation. This means no swearing, no physical violence (which falls under the safety issue also), no vicious name-calling or obvious backtalk. It also means being kind to animals and Mother Earth.

My second list, which consists of behaviors that I don't like but will tolerate, consists mainly of appearances. I don't always appreciate what either of my children wear, but over the years I have learned to tolerate their choices in clothing and hairstyle for the sake of peace. As long as the look is temporary, which means no tattoos or body piercings, they can dress or wear their hair the way they want. The exception to this would be if what they wear violates the dress code policy at school. Some of the other not-so-wonderful behaviors I tolerate include messy bedrooms and how they spend their free time.

My third list consists of behaviors I'll negotiate. For example, I often bargain over time spent chauffering Brandan around. As a general rule, if he has been generally well behaved, I will offer to take him and his friends to the mall or movies. However, if he is grumpy or argumentative and requests a ride somewhere, I refuse to budge. Overall, I think it is a good idea to put as many behaviors in this third column as possible. It is always good to have a bargaining chip up your sleeve if you need one. Children also cooperate much better when they know their reward is dependent on their behavior.

While Dr. Greene's idea of using the lists does form a wonderful outline in assisting parents when to draw the line, knowing when to make an issue out of a behavior is still something that each and every parent must decide for themselves. It is not something that can be read in a book or taught overnight. It is just one of those things that comes with knowing your child. And although whether or not to go to battle over something can seem like an agonizing decision, it is rarely a life or death situation. No war has ever really been won or lost on just one or two battlefields. When it comes down to it, it is the overall resolution and connection of the troops that really matters.

11
Staying Connected

Kurt Angle swings Chris Jericho over his shoulder and drops him like a bag of cement. Stephanie moans at the sight. Throwing back her long black hair in a sweep, she jumps into the center of the action. Triple H, Stephanie's ex-husband, quickly pursues her. Before Triple H can get to her though, she jumps on Angle's back and begins pounding him on the head. Just as Triple H reaches her, Jericho get up from the floor and grabs him around the waist. Both men fly over the side of the stage and onto the floor with a thud. Angle picks up a chair and begins swinging.

Ten-year-old Brandan moves closer to the TV set to get a better look. In an attempt to act equally enthralled I, too, scoot forward. Thursday night SmackDown! is serious business at our house. Actually, everything that has to do with World Wrestling Entertainment is serious business to Brandan. But since he is only allowed to watch wrestling two hours a week, SmackDown! is especially important.

"Did you see that hit?" Brandan shouts.

I nod and think about how much wrestling has in common with *Jerry Springer*. My husband and I actually abhor the sport, but we know how important it is to Brandan. So rather than disconnect from it, and him, we have resigned ourselves to watching it with him once a week.

"Look what he does now," Brandan says, making sure that my attention doesn't wander.

I reiterate my wrestling mom mantra. "I see that, but remember none of it is real. They are acting."

Brandan, of course, knows this, as we've discussed it a thousand times. Still, he behaves as though two superheroes are battling it out for control of the free world.

A tall blond girl enters the ring. "Who's she?" I ask suspiciously. Lately, I can't help but notice that more and more women are involved in wrestling. And these aren't just any women. They are steroid-saturated Barbie doll clones. Twelve-inch waists. Forty-inch busts. Arms and calves like Arnold Schwarzenegger. On top of that, they don't exactly look like they are dressed for combat. One of them appears to be wearing clothes that were hand painted on. In addition to worrying about the violence, I begin to worry about the sexual stimulation wrestling has on my son's already heightened hormone levels.

"That's Stephanie's arch rival, Stacy Keibler," Brandan chirps.

I can see that my son definitely knows his stuff. This girl immediately tackles Stephanie and they fall to the floor with a thud. This is not a usual catfight. These women certainly know some moves. I am appalled at my interest in the fact that they are even in the ring. Yet as the match goes on, I find myself being drawn to it. No wonder wrestling is such big business; it is oddly addicting.

"Can we build a wrestling ring in the backyard?" Brandan asks.

My mind conjures up a makeshift ring consisting of a blanket and a few wooden posts tied together by rope. "Sure," I answer. "You and your friends can put one together this weekend."

Brandan looks annoyed. "I mean a real one."

"NO!" My husband answers. I can't help but laugh at the thought of a professional wrestling ring in our backyard. But Brandan will not be sidetracked.

"Please! Since I'm going to be a wrestler when I grow up, I won't be needing my college fund."

"No!" my husband and I answer in unison.

Brandan folds his arms in indignation, but his bad mood over the decision quickly dissipates as the next round starts. He snatches a four-foot-long body pillow off the couch and wrestles it to the ground. Because he is forbidden from wrestling anything with a pulse, this poor pillow has become the subject of his assaults.

We continue to watch the matches, and the silly sideshow bantering that goes on in between them. A part of me wants to change the channels on the TV and in Brandan's brain. But the other part of me knows that in order to stay connected to my son, I have to be a part of his world. And for the moment at least, his world includes two hours a week of the WWE.

IN ADDITION TO knowing the semantics of World Wrestling Entertainment, I am also fluent in football, basketball, baseball, soccer, and hockey, none of which I knew anything about before I became Brandan's mother. I can recite Brandan's favorite color, song, and teacher, the name of his crush on any given day, along with how many pairs of clean underwear he has in the second drawer of his dresser. I also know how many loose teeth he has, when the last time he washed his hair was, and what he had for lunch at school. If Brandan were a quiz I would score 100.

I am proud of my status as a Brandan Boylan expert. For my proficiency in my son is my backstage pass to his world. It is also the rope that keeps me tethered to his speeding boat. And the small, seeming insignificant trivia that I know about Brandan is the fiber that makes up this connection.

I realize that some might say that this link is really just the umbilical cord that never got snipped, and that my apron strings are the only things keeping Brandan and I close. I don't care. My goal is to help direct Brandan's wild spirit and at the same time keep it free. Despite what the bystanders might have to say about being overly involved, overly protective, and overly intrusive, my strategy to stay connected does work. It gives me access to areas of his heart and mind that are not privy to the outside world, and it allows me to catch a glimpse of all his magical adventures.

My link to Brandan also allows me to look ahead and view the impending obstructions that litter his waterway. I am able to foresee potential problems before they happen. That doesn't, of course, mean that I always intervene on Brandan's behalf. Nor does it mean that I attempt to divert him from the inevitable disasters. I am quite aware that Brandan will have to learn most of his lessons the hard way. What being in step with him does mean is that I am able to brace myself for the bumps along the way. I am able to protect myself and the rest of the family from the fallout from his freshest fiasco.

By staying connected to Brandan, I am also able to predict what discussions need to be instigated earlier than normal. For highly active children are precocious in many areas, and they unexpectedly reach milestones before their peers. A perfect example of this would be Brandan's curiosity for the opposite sex. Brandan started noticing, thinking about, and generally obsessing about girls long before any other of the boys his age. Because I was in sync with the direction he was headed, my husband and I were able to intercede and speak with him about sexual issues years before we normally would have. If our connection hadn't been there, I probably never would have realized that he had reached that point so early. I doubt that Brandan would have felt comfortable confiding in me about his feelings, either.

Bumping along behind Brandan's boat is not as easy as it sounds, though. He frequently changes courses abruptly and without warning. Though he is fixated on the WWE today, that may not be the case for long. In fact, by the time this book has gone to press, wrestling will be old news at the Boylan house. Nevertheless, in an effort to hold up my end of the connection, I resign myself to remaining flexible and open to his latest craze. I read *Harry Potter* and *Fishing World Magazine*. I watch *SpongeBob SquarePants, Greg the Bunny* and *Grounded for Life*. I learn wrestling moves and how to do "the worm." I listen to Creed and Smash Mouth. Most important, I get to know Brandan's friends, and I make a concerted effort to speak their language.

On top of all of this, I know that things are only going to get worse over the coming years. In many ways, I am in a race against time. Now that Brandan is entering his teenage years, remaining connected will become an uphill battle. Although he loves being with me now, I am certain that this will not always be the case. In fact, I know that now that Brandan is eleven, my days as his expert are numbered. Pretty soon, he will stop sharing information, stop confiding, and stop wanting to be around me. In essence, I will get the proverbial boot. My only hope is to build as strong a bond as I possibly can, so that the disconnections, when they come, will be short-lived and easy to repair.

My mastermind plan to stay connected to Brandan starts with being physically present in his life now. Although the phrase "quality time" has become quite popular, I don't believe it applies to highly active children. Quantity is more important than quality when it comes to dealing with a child who would just as soon burn the house down as not. Being physically available for these children is just not an option; it is a necessity if they are going to stay safe. But even after they have matured and are able to be left alone for extended periods of time, being present has many emotional advantages as well.

When Brandan was first taken off of Ritalin, I spent every afternoon playing a short game of football with him on the front lawn. My husband also took at least thirty minutes every day to participate with him in some sort of physical activity. I truly believe that these two thirty-minute sessions of physical interaction every day, along with our continual presence at home, became the glue that kept Brandan together during a very difficult time. It also healed his mind as well as his body in a way that no medicine or therapy could have. In looking back, it must have looked silly to the neighbors, a forty-year-old mother rolling around in the grass and dirt with her eight-year-old son. But the return on my emotional and physical investment turned out to be well worth any temporary humiliation.

Another physical ritual, which also turned out to have emotional benefits as well, was bedtime. Every evening until the time both my children were nine or ten, I would lie down beside them until they fell asleep. Most nights I did it out of sheer exhaustion from fighting the late-night curtain calls and other bedtime battles that children go through. There were also many nights when I did it because I wanted to. There is something magical about the darkness and eerie quietness of the night that causes a child to want to confess every thought that is going through his or her mind. Both my children would tell me secrets that they never would have confided in the light of day. Despite the warning by a prominent psychologist that I was doing irreparable damage to them, both my son and my daughter eventually outgrew this ritual and now go to sleep on their own. I have since attempted to find another experience to replace it, but I have yet to find anything that bonded us as tightly and as effortlessly as this one did.

In addition to being physically present for Brandan, I have also tried to be emotionally and spiritually available for him. I have been willing to share what I know to be true about life with my son. I have also been willing to disclose my own emotions and feelings. When a dear cousin of mine died, I allowed myself to sob openly in front of Brandan. My tears and emotions provided a wonderful springboard for us to discuss death and grief, and what happens to our souls when our bodies die. In addition to permitting my son to witness my emotions, I also allow him to share his. Most highly active children have very strong emotions, and Brandan is no exception. He cries more, laughs harder, gets frustrated easier, and is generally more sentimental than other boys his age. However, no matter how dramatic or histrionic he may seem, I encourage him to share his feelings as openly and as often as he needs to.

While the physical and emotional bond is extremely important to the parent-child relationship, neither one is nearly as effective or as fulfilling as the spiritual connection. In fact, I believe that being fashioned by the spirit is really the basis of all other human connections. The joining of two souls, whether they be mother and son, mother and father, or sister and brother, transcends all other experiences. Spiritual harmony brings a sense of peace that smooths over everything from conflicts about curfews to bath-time brawls. In essence, a spiritual connection occurs on a much deeper level, and it not only becomes the filament that brings the two souls together, but it becomes the basis for a deeper relationship with a third party—God. This third relationship then cements the link, binding the souls even when they are emotionally and or physically disengaged.

One of the best ways for staying spiritually connected with a child is through prayer and meditation. Whether it is done in the morning, at meal time, or right before bed, a child of any age can be taught the importance of conversing with his creator. That means that not only does he set time aside to speak to God, but he takes time out of his day to listen. In order for a child to understand the concept of prayer, though, he or she needs to hear others pray. The mechanics of prayer and meditation are not taught, they are demonstrated. I've always felt that the most intimate time for praying, and for listening, is at bedtime. These added moments of quiet bring a certain reverence to the ritual. They also bring a sense of peace to a child who is strung out from a long and busy day. When Brandan was a small child, he loved to pray. He wasn't all that adept at listening, but he loved to recite prayers, especially before mealtime. Although now that he is older he prefers to pray "in his head," he still enjoys listening to me pray out loud.

Another equally important activity is attending worship service together. Highly active children love to congregate, and religious assemblies are no exception. Attending services together also opens the door to an ongoing discussion on theological and philosophical beliefs between parent and child. In addition to bringing a parent and child closer together spiritually, attending services gives them added time to connect physically and emotionally.

That doesn't mean that forging a spiritual bond has to be an organized event, though. It can be done anywhere, anyplace, and anytime. A walk in the park or a trip to the zoo can be a springboard to discussing beliefs about God and the universe. Even the death of a beloved family member, as tragic as it may seem at the time, is an opportunity to start a conversation about God. I believe that the most important thing to remember about engaging spiritually with a child, is that, like physically bonding, it must be ongoing. A parent can't just make a quick connection now and then. In order to keep the link strong through the teen years, parents must make a continual effort to keep the lines of spiritual communication open. They must be committed to nourishing their child's spirits with rituals and open conversation as well as trips to the local church, synagogue, or mosque.

As I continue to physically, emotionally, and spiritually build that bridge between my world and my son's, I also try to remember that connecting doesn't mean controlling. Although Brandan and I have a tightly knitted bond, I don't feel as though I must be cemented to his every move. I like to think of our connection as more of a square knot, loose but secure. I want to keep our relationship intact, but I don't want to smother him to the point that I am his sole support. I want him to feel free to speed along on his merry way without always looking over his shoulder.

When it comes right down to it, I guess what I really want is for Brandan's spirit to be free but obtainable. This is, of course, truly the paradox to fostering a long and sturdy bond of trust with a highly active child. For to be truly connected means mastering the art of holding on tightly to a rope while at the same time pretending that it isn't even there. It means being invisibly present in all his activities. It means dramatically spilling my guts while at the same time learning how to keep my emotional distance. It also means spiritually giving him all that I have, and then letting him make his own decision about God. I guess I could sum it by saying that keeping that connection means working tirelessly to capture my son's heart, mind, and spirit only to turn around and set them free again.

12

Teaching Self-Monitoring Skills

The buzzing of the alarm clock jolts me from a dead sleep. I hate mornings, especially dark, cold, rainy mornings. I force myself out of bed and up the staircase to Brandan's new room. We moved his bed and all of his belongings out of the tiny bedroom and into the spacious game room last week under the agreement that he would be more responsible for himself. This means, of course, that he must set his own alarm and get himself up and ready for school in the morning without being called. It is day three, and he has already reneged on his promise. Not only is he still in bed, but he is practically comatose.

Now that Brandan is entering the preteen years, his eagerness to get up and get going in the morning has taken a backseat to his need for sleep. Never having been a morning person myself, I can't really blame him for wanting to stay in bed. But consistently being late in our school district not only gets you a tardy slip, it can also land you a monetary fine.

I make my way over to Brandan's bed, and though I am tempted to crawl in next to him, I shake him awake. "Get up. It's time for school."

Brandan peers at me through one eye, and then looks around the room in disbelief. "What time is it?"

"Seven o'clock. You must have turned your alarm off again." I strip the covers from him, forcing him to curl up in a tight ball on the bed. "Get up!"

I turn to leave. The alarm clock is definitely not working for Brandan. I wonder if I am setting it too early for him. Too many hits on the snooze button and it turns off completely. I make a mental note to set it fifteen minutes later tomorrow morning. If that doesn't work, I'll switch alarms with him and see if he responds better to mine.

Once downstairs, I head for the kitchen. Although Brandan is capable of making his own breakfast, his culinary skills are so messy that I have decided not to add cooking to his list of things he must do for himself.

I fix Brandan a bagel with cream cheese, and return to the bottom of the stairs to call his name. There is no response. Obviously, my plan to make him more responsible is not working. I trek back up the stairs. Much to my surprise, though, Brandan is out of bed, dressed, and is putting on his shoes. I am impressed, and compliment him on his choice of clothing.

Brandan eats breakfast while watching cartoons. I refrain from commenting on the fact that time is slipping by and that he will be late if he doesn't hurry. With five minutes to spare, he notices the time on his own and heads to the bathroom to brush his teeth. I lurk quietly outside to see if he is following the checklist that is taped to the mirror.

I composed several itemized lists on index cards of all the things Brandan has to complete throughout the day and posted them around the house. He is embarrassed by all the lists and refuses to acknowledge that he reads them. However, by the way he is following them down to the letter, I can see that he is referring to them religiously. The four-by-six card taped to the bathroom mirror reads: brush teeth for two minutes, gargle, put on deodorant, comb hair. Brandan sets the egg timer by the sink for two minutes and picks up his toothbrush. After spreading far too much toothpaste on the bristles, he jams the appliance into his mouth. The short, rapid back-and-forth movement promptly brings on an excess of foam that cascades onto his chin. When the allotted two minutes is up, Brandan spits the glob of frothy bubbles into the sink and completes the remainder of his routine before exiting the bathroom. On the way out he stumbles over me in the hallway. I immediately pretend to be busy with something else. Amanda, who is directly behind me, points out the toothpaste on her brother's chin.

Brandan ignores her and puts on his jacket and backpack. I offer to take him to school, but the rain has temporarily stopped and he volunteers to ride his bike. He glances at the list that is posted by the front entrance:

homework, lunch money, bike lock, wallet, comb, back-pack, helmet. He is out the door and down the sidewalk before I can blink. Maybe the plan is working after all.

By three o'clock Brandan is home again, watching TV on the couch with his best friend. I ask him if he has any homework. He shakes his head no. Because homework is not sent home every day, I am not sure if he is lying or not. I decide to temporarily let it slide on the off bet that he is telling the truth.

I leave the house to pick up my daughter from school, leaving Brandan with strict instructions NOT to make a mess while I am gone. When I return Brandan and his friend are nowhere to be seen. Muffin crumbs and plastic wrappers form a trail from the kitchen to the family room, telling me that he was there. I hear noises coming from his bedroom and call for him to come down. He immediately appears at the top of the stairs.

"What's wrong?" he asks. I am still amazed at how shortsighted he can be.

"There are wrappers on the floor in the kitchen," I say.

"Oh," he says, looking sheepish.

I turn and go back to the kitchen to wait. When he doesn't come down within the next two minutes, I trek back up the stairs and ask his friend to leave.

Brandan immediately begins pleading. "Why does he have to leave?"

"I told you there are crumbs and trash all over the kitchen."

Brandan looks perplexed. "You didn't tell us to clean it up."

"If you are self-monitoring yourself, then I shouldn't have to tell you." I insist again that his friend go home. Brandan stomps down the stairs and slams the door behind his buddy. I remind him that we have a deal that if he wants more responsibility, he is going to have to look after himself. He storms into the kitchen, disposes the trash, and disappears into his room.

I vacillate between feeling guilty and self-righteous about sending his friend home, and am relieved when Brandan finally comes downstairs with a smile on his face. "Got any homework?" I ask again.

"Yes and no," he answers, turning on the TV.

I immediately stop what I am doing and position myself in front of the set. "What is that supposed to mean?"

Brandan leans back on the couch and casually puts his hands behind his head. He gives me one of those lopsided grins that melts my heart and makes anything he says sound logical. "I have homework, but I'm using my homework pass that I got in class today for being so good so I don't really have to do any work."

I ignore the grin and attempt to comprehend what he just said. He did something good at school today. He received a homework pass as a reward. He wants to use the pass tonight to get out of doing his homework. I understand his excuse, but wonder if I should argue the point. Truly he should not be wasting the homework pass already. All the reasons why he should wait and save it for an emergency run through my mind. What if he gets sick? What if something comes up and he can't get to his homework? What if he has homework that he doesn't understand? Besides all the catastrophic possibilities of why he may need the pass, there's also the fact that there's no reason why he shouldn't be studying now. After all, he has nothing else to do. I hold my tongue for a minute and try to word my suggestion carefully.

With eerie foresight I ask, "What happens if you can't do your homework because of basketball practice tomorrow night?"

Brandan shifts his body so that he can see around me. "I'll do it before practice."

I resist debating the obvious reasons for making him do his homework, instead of watching television, and leave him to make his own mistakes. By now I know that Brandan is just one of those kids who has to learn his lessons the hard way.

That night at dinner I position a giant mirror across the kitchen table from Brandan, which is immediately questioned by everyone in the family. "I think we all need to brush up on our manners, and I read that the best way to do that is to watch yourself eat," I announce. "Everyone will have a turn at eating in front of the mirror. Brandan is first."

I can see that Brandan thinks this is a cool idea by the huge grin on his face. He starts by flinging a forkful of mashed potatoes into his mouth. A small dab of white mush drips onto his chin. He smiles at himself and wipes it off with his sleeve. My husband starts to correct him, but I nudge him under the table. It is important that Brandan notice and correct his mistakes on his own without having to be told. Brandan's sister comments that this is the most absurd thing she has ever heard of and points out that it doesn't seem to be helping her brother at all.

Meanwhile, Brandan continues to watch himself eat with great amazement. It's as if he is accomplishing the task of eating for the first time. For the first ten minutes he consistently chews with his mouth wide open, just for the shock value. When he finally reaches the point of disgusting even himself, he becomes more conscientious about his manners. By the end of the meal, I notice that he is much more aware of his eating habits than when he started. He notices when he drops food. He closes his mouth when he eats. He even remembers to cut his meat properly. I pat myself on the back for such an ingenious idea and remind myself to pull the mirror out periodically.

Brandan completes his nightly routine with relative ease. The next morning, he is up with his alarm and ready for school. However, he ignores the list by the door and subsequently forgets his bike lock. Five minutes later he is back in the house searching for it. I remind him for the up-teenth time to look at the list.

That afternoon he comes home from school, immediately deposits his backpack by the door, and announces that he has to start a project over at a friend's house. This particular friend is a girl, and I can see that he is more excited about going to her house then he is about the project itself. He promises to be back by dinnertime and slams the door on the way out.

While he is gone, I sneak a peek in his backpack. It looks like he has some serious math homework in addition to studying his spelling words. I immediately start to ruminate about how I should have made more of an issue out of saving the homework pass. Leaving Brandan to monitor himself is much more difficult than I imagined.

By the time Brandan has finished his project and made his way back home, it is dinnertime. After dinner, it is off to basketball practice. Getting to and from the gym, in addition to the period spent on the court, takes at least two hours. We arrive back home just as it is time to get ready for bed. I am sure that Brandan will remember his homework, but he doesn't. At ten o'clock, just as he is dozing off to sleep, he jumps out of his bed and runs downstairs. "I have homework!" he screams.

I resist the urge to chide him about wasting his pass or to panic with him, and calmly suggest he get started.

Brandan immediately scrambles for his backpack and a pencil. Ten minutes into the work, he starts to complain. "I am too tired to finish."

Instead of offering sympathy, I suggest that he go to bed and get up early to complete the work.

"I can't," he protests. "I'll be too tired in the morning!"

I ignore his whining and get ready for bed myself. By eleven o'clock he is finished. He trudges up the stairs as though both of his legs are made of lead. The next morning not only does he not get up for his alarm, but he refuses to get out of bed all together.

I try getting my catatonic son up by pulling him out from under the covers by his feet and throwing a wet rag on his face. It doesn't work. I try goading him with his favorite breakfast—bacon and eggs. It doesn't help. I resort to threats and screaming. It only makes matters worse. Brandan eventually does get out of bed, but not until twenty minutes after class has started. I doubt the usefulness of the self-monitoring theory; however, I am determined to give it at least two weeks before I make a decision one way or the other.

The next several days are like the first few. Brandan erratically and inconsistently monitors himself. He forgets to put his science homework in his bag, and subsequently gets a zero on the paper. He loses the key to his bike lock. He leaves his math book at school. He wakes up to his alarm only half the time. I abandon my attempts to get him up altogether, and instead let him face the consequences of being tardy. Although I am discouraged, I am still determined to follow through with my plan.

Much to my surprise and pleasure, the following week is much better. Brandan remembers all of his homework, gets himself up on time, and does his chores without being prompted. The bonus is that I am no longer considered the ogre in the family. My voice no longer sounds hoarse from yelling up the stairs, and my nerves are finally starting to settle after eleven years of being on edge.

Over the next year or so, Brandan slips up more than a few times, but in general, showing him how to self-monitor rates high on my scale of freeing his spirit.

VERY FEW CHILDREN are able to monitor their daily self-care activities without some prompting. Most need to be reminded now and then to brush their teeth, do their homework, and clean their rooms, and they occasionally tend to forget things and lose track of time. But for the most part, they carry with them an innate sense of their surroundings and the effect that their actions have on others. Highly active children, on the other hand, are on the extreme end of the self-care spectrum. Activities such as brushing their teeth, remembering their backpacks, and managing time seem insurmountable to a child whose thoughts are a million light-years away.

I have heard many educators say that highly active children live in a different world. The truth is that most of these children do. Because they always see the bigger picture, they aren't aware of the smaller, more mundane intricacies of life, such as table manners and being on time. They aren't aware of the fact that they are acting in an annoying or abrasive manner. More important, they aren't always aware of the consequences that result from their indifference to these details.

Highly active children do not come equipped with an inherent sense of their immediate surroundings the way the rest of us do. In many ways they just aren't as sensitive to tiny nuances as the average person. The fact that a tablespoon of mashed potatoes, or toothpaste, is dripping from their chins doesn't matter when their minds are on the baseball game they're going to be playing the following week. This doesn't mean that highly active children aren't perceptive. On the contrary, spirited children are very intuitive and insightful individuals. It's just that their perceptions are directed on a more global level.

Over the years I have tried several different strategies to make Brandan more cognizant of his immediate surroundings. I have nagged him about his table manners and personal hygiene. I have literally taken him by the hand and walked him through each step. I have even done what I call running interference—which pretty much means completing the job for him.

When it came down to it, though, none of these tactics really worked. Nagging Brandan simply made him more determined not to do the assignment. Walking him through each step only kept his attention for the required amount of time. Although doing his work for him did get the task completed, continuously running interference for another human being is exhausting. Eventually I came to understand that, whether he was highly active or not, Brandan was still going to have to follow directions and complete certain assignments on his own in order to be successful. And so, the old saying of "give a man a fish and it will feed him for a day; teach a man to fish and he eats for a lifetime" became my mantra.

In the beginning though, teaching a highly active child how to fish for himself can be quite demanding. In fact the majority of those first few weeks are often spent reeling in empty lines. During his initiation period, the spirited child is also forced to taste a bit of his own bitter bait, so to speak, by experiencing the direct consequences of his actions. Furthermore, it takes a lot of patience on the part of a parent to sit by and watch their impulsive, easily distractible child struggle with the everyday activities that other children seem to complete with very little effort. It is important to remember, though, that as difficult as it is to train a spirited child, it is just as hard on the child to be trained. It takes a lot of patience and determination on his part to slow himself down long enough to attend to life's little details.

Unfortunately, children who are highly active have an aversion to attending to details. I have heard many experts say that this is because their brain activity is slower. These experts claim that the slower than normal brain activity is what hinders children who have been labeled as ADHD from being attentive and focused. But again, I don't think that this so-called inattentiveness or distractibility is due to sluggish brain activity. Nor do I think that these children are deficient in the area of awareness or alertness. In fact, I believe it is the exact opposite. I believe that a child's inability to attend to details is due to the fact that he is aware of so many occurrences, that the brain simply makes the decision to ignore some things and focus in on others.

The real solution then is to teach a child when it is appropriate to allow his mind to expand and include the bigger picture, such as during sports and other physical or creative activities, and when it is necessary to rein the brain in and focus on the smaller more mundane issues, such as remembering to put his napkin in his lap at mealtime. Of course, highly active children not only need to be taught how to rein in their brains, but they also need to be instructed on how to keep their brains in gear until the required task is completed.

Again, this is not easy. Highly active children have minds that are used to wandering, and subsequently they get bored easily. But like any skill, teaching a child how to focus for sustained periods of time can be mastered. The brain itself is a creature of habit. Thoughts and feelings flow in the direction of least resistance, and once a child's mind is taught to focus on specific details, it is more likely to do so in the future.

In training the brain, it is sometimes necessary to incorporate outside tools to assist a child in monitoring himself. That doesn't mean, of course, that a parent should run interference. The tools should come in the form of prompters that the child can utilize on his own. I have provided Brandan with daily, monthly, and weekly calendars to plan his extracurricular activities as well as his schoolwork. He also has an ample supply of Post-It notes that he can use as reminders.

Before a parent goes out and stocks up on office supplies and other tools for their child, though, they should outline all their expectations—the more specifics the better. Because highly active children simply do not have the innate understanding and logic that goes with attending to details, the expectations of chores, responsibilities, and general hygiene must be spelled out for them. It is not enough to tell a highly active child to clean his room. The definitions of a clean room must be clarified. Detailed instructions, such as make the bed, pick up all the paper on the floor, place the dirty clothes in hamper, and organize the toys, are essential. It is important to remember that highly active children truly get the bigger picture of how life works, which keeps them from understanding how to put the smaller picture together. Getting the details down on paper is vital to helping them.

Over the years I have found checklists to be indispensable. Not only do the written lists clarify expectations for Brandan, but they also clarify expectations for me. Because written lists constitute a binding agreement at our house, once a chore is listed, I am bound by contract not to do it for Brandan. My assistance is no longer under discussion. There is to be no nagging and no running interference on my part. If the list says that Brandan is responsible for getting his backpack ready, then he is expected to do it. It clearly says so on the list, and I am not to feel guilty if he forgets to pack it properly. Most important, I do not have to listen to Brandan whine if it doesn't get done.

I have found that in the beginning it is better not to be too heavy-handed in dolling out responsibilities, especially if a child is used to his parents reminding him or running interference. Children can feel overwhelmed and out of control if too much responsibility is turned over to them all at once. Basic tasks such as hygiene, schoolwork, and getting up and dressed without being called should be first on the list. As a child learns to complete these assignments with ease, more responsibilities can be added.

The second step in teaching a highly active child to self-monitor is to make sure that there is an understanding on the part of everyone involved that life will probably be very chaotic for the first few weeks. In order to truly allow a child to self-monitor, a parent must be willing to allow for the consequences. These consequences usually involve a messy household, missed appointments, tardies at school, slipping grades, and lots and lots of disagreements. It is only natural that the highly active child will make a lot of mistakes on his road to freedom. Items will be lost or misplaced, deadlines and dates will be missed, and life can become downright disastrous when a child is expected to monitor himself. Tempting as it is, it is imperative that parents and other bystanders not jump in and assist the child. In fact, it is important from the get-go to make it clear to everyone involved that chaos will prevail until the child has mastered the desired skills.

This means letting the school in on the fact that the child may be late and disorganized for a few weeks or months. The child, of course, should still be held accountable for his actions. He or she will get tardy slips, zeroes on incomplete papers, and so on. It's just that warning the teachers and other adults beforehand at least lets them know that there is a new approach at home that will spill out into other areas. Occasionally, a parent may have a hard time getting a teacher or other school personnel to cooperate. A few educators still feel that parents should force a child into compliance. But as long as there is a time limit on how long a child will be allowed to go without some interference, most teachers will go along with the plan.

The last step is to follow through. Setting a child's spirit free is never an easy task. In fact, loosening the ropes, whether it be done by switching schools, rebounding from Ritalin, or strengthening self-monitoring skills, can be a very scary experience for everyone involved. It can also be quite heartbreaking. During the time it took me to free Brandan's spirit, I cried a river of tears, turned gray-headed, and literally chewed all my nails down to the nub. There were also many mornings when, for the sake of everyone's sanity, I was tempted to give up on my plan to teach Brandan how to self-monitor. Overall, it would have been much easier on me to simply complete the assignments myself then to stand by and idly watch his life spin out of control. Somehow we all kept going until self-monitoring finally became second nature to Brandan. In retrospect I'm glad we did.

In addition to teaching him responsibility, self-monitoring slowed Brandan's brain down long enough for him to focus on and appreciate the smaller, more beautiful details of life, and it instilled in him a sense of pride that he never would have achieved if I had continued to run interference.

Turning the reins over to Brandan also taught me that being a responsible parent doesn't mean I have to control his every move, nor do I have to micromanage every detail of his life. In fact, the whole experience of teaching Brandan to self-monitor reminded me of the old saying that from the moment our children are born, our jobs as parents is to begin letting go.

13

Improving Listening Skills

Like a moth in a cocoon, I am immobilized. Except for my head and toes, my entire body is swaddled in a thick layer of sheets and blankets. The cool air breezes over my face, reminding me that nothing is more sinfully relaxing than being able to sleep in on a weekday morning; especially when the morning is wintery cold. I tilt my face toward the clock. It is almost 10 A.M. New Year's Day, and I don't have to be anywhere for the next twenty-four hours. The cozy sensation of the bedcovers wrapped tightly around my torso makes me feel like a fat bear in the middle of hibernation. I revel in the feeling and wonder if I can come up with an excuse to remain here for the entire day. From my bed I see that yesterday's snowfall is still blanketing the trees and grass in the backyard. The postcard view of this winter wonderland further relaxes me. It is a rare occasion in Texas to have a mix of sleet and ice, much less get such an abundant drift of real snow. It is even more unusual to have the powdery stuff around for more than a day.

Suddenly, high pitched screams from outside the house interrupt my thoughts. A child is obviously in distress, and I can be assured that somehow my ten-year-old son is involved in the altercation. I decide to temporarily abandon my short-lived sanctuary and investigate. Wrapped in a sufficient surplus of blankets, I maneuver my way into the living room, spread the slats of the blinds with my thumb and forefinger, and peer onto the front lawn. Oddly enough, the screams are coming from Brandan, who is diligently dodging snowballs in the yard. Two boys across the street are catapulting their crystallized ammunition at our house. From the limited view that I have, I notice that the boys are not from our neighborhood. I also notice that Brandan is wearing a pair of mittens and his *SpongeBob SquarePants* hat, but no coat.

I knock on the glass pane. Brandan doesn't hear me, of course. His screams, along with those of his opponents, muffle the faint taps. The other boys, who are properly bundled in heavy winter coats and scarves in addition to mittens and caps, have advanced on Brandan and are now hurling snowballs from the sidewalk. I decide that I should make Brandan come inside and put on his coat before the battle gets serious. Still wrapped in my blankets, I make my way to the foyer, taking tiny, baby-like steps as I go. I crack the door and stick my head out. A blast of arctic air hits me in the face.

"It is freezing outside," I squeak. "Where is your coat?"

Brandan continues with his mission as though he didn't hear a thing. He darts around the tree with giant snowballs in each hand. Winding up his arm like a pitcher on the mound, he lets one rip. The powdery ball finds a mark on the back of his opponent's head and explodes into a million tiny flakes. The shrieks of laughter from Brandan drown out the screams of indignation from the wounded enemy as they both run for cover.

I am tempted to watch the Siberian warfare, but am reminded of the warm bed that is waiting, and the fact that Brandan is coatless in twenty-degree weather. I repeat my directive, louder this time. There is no response. Although I have had Brandan's hearing checked no less than half a dozen times since he was three, I can't help but wonder if he is going deaf. I give him the benefit of the doubt and try again. This time I push open the front door and reposition my pajama-clad, blanket-encased torso in full view.

"You are going to catch pneumonia if you don't put your coat on!" I scream. I throw a warning about frostbite in for good measure.

Normally, any warning that involves serious illness and the loss of body parts has a way of making a child pay attention. Today, however, the admonition of death and/or frozen limbs has no effect at all. Brandan continues to dash back and forth, dodging his foe's slick arsenal of snow, dirt, and dead grass. His shirt and pants, damp from the bombardment of snowballs, cling to his body like a wetsuit. Several neighborhood boys have now joined in the war, and are helping Brandan fight off the interlopers. Everyone but Brandan is properly dressed for combat.

I decide to use my broken-record technique. "Brandan, come inside. Brandan, come inside. Brandan, come inside." Brandan immediately stops in his tracks and turns in the direction of my voice. As he does, a snowball whizzes past him and splatters against the door, three inches from my head. Tiny bits of frost cover my blanket and my face. The offending child looks horrified, and there is momentary silence from everyone. Finally, Brandan acknowledges my presence. "Look, Mom, the snow's still here!" He then promptly picks up a clump of white stuff off the ground and hurls it at the enemy.

"I see that! Now come put on a jacket or you are going to be too sick to play in it tomorrow!" I scream. But it is too late. The brief moment of having Brandan's undivided attention dissolved the minute I stopped being target practice.

I dust the snow from my blanket and debate my next move. I am incredibly annoyed at the fact that Brandan is so oblivious to me. Why doesn't he just stop what he is doing, come inside, and put on his coat? My bare toes curl against the fallen bits of ice. My teeth begin to chatter. More than likely, I am the one who will get frostbite. I want to go back to my bed where it is warm and cozy. Maybe I should surrender to the inevitable, and allow Brandan to run amok in the snow without a coat.

I try to convince myself that being outside in freezing temperatures without a coat is not so bad. After all, if he were really cold, he would have come inside already. Wouldn't he? My maternal instinct intersects this rationale, and I weigh the alternative. What if he really does become deathly ill from frostbite or pneumonia? I finally conclude that the guilt from ignoring the situation would probably keep me from resting anyway, and decide to give it one more try.

Only this time I scream my directive at the top of my lungs. For some reason, it always seems to work for my husband. Both of my children respond better to their father than to me. I try to make my voice sound deep, and as loud and as menacing as I possibly can. "If you don't put your coat on, then you are going to have to come inside for the rest of the day."

Brandan dashes out toward the sidewalk without complying. He reaches up and snatches his *SpongeBob SquarePants* hat off of his head and begins shoveling snow into it.

Finally, I reach the end of my rope and shed my blankets. Braving the slippery sidewalk, I trek out to where Brandan is standing and grab him by the back of his snow-drenched shirt. With the power and strength that only an exhausted mother standing barefoot in her pajamas in the middle of her front yard during a snowstorm can have, I give Brandan a swift jerk. His face, beet red from the arctic air, or vigorous activity, or maybe both, twists around to me in amazement. "Mom," he asks, eyeing me suspiciously, "what are you doing outside dressed like that?"

THE INABILITY TO listen, which is of course actually the inability to pay attention, is a problem that plagues all children. It is a problem that also afflicts quite a few adults. In fact, a lack of listening skills is one of the most frequent complaints from everyone in the entire family. Husbands ignore their wives. Wives don't pay attention to the needs of their husbands. Teenagers complain that their parents don't listen to them. Parents say that their children won't follow their advice. As a society we have become a group of people who knowingly and willingly shut out the voices, opinions, and requests of those who matter to us the most. And, like many other of society's ills, this flaw is magnified in highly active children.

Spirited children are born with a talent for turning a deaf ear to the opinions, voices, reasoning, and warnings of adults. In fact one might even say they are gifted in the art of ignoring. They also have an uncanny, and quite annoying, way of making it seem as though the speaker had never uttered a word.

Although it seems like a minor flaw, having inadequate listening skills can pose serious problems. For one, a child's irritating ingenuity for sidestepping even the smallest and easiest of directives is enough to push even the most patient of parents and caregivers over the edge. Brandan's tendency to tune me out has at times made me literally want to pull out every hair on my head, and his along with it. I'm not alone in my frustration. I have heard many parents of highly active children state that they have wondered at some time or another whether their child was partially deaf. The listening skills of highly active students is also, without a doubt, one of the most talked about complaints from teachers and educators.

In fact, selective hearing can become so exaggerated that it interferes with a caregiver's ability to communicate effectively with the child. A child who cannot follow the simplest of directives finds himself at a big disadvantage. His lack of listening skills not only affects his relationship with his parents and his teachers, but it influences his relationship with his peers. When a child stops listening, he stops connecting. He then begins to shut out the world altogether. And a child who is alienated can never be truly free. The inability to have meaningful relationships will bind him tighter than any rope ever could. It will also cause scars that no amount of freedom can rectify.

I knew from the moment that I decided to set Brandan's spirit free that in order for him to survive in the world, he was going to have to learn to listen, not only to me, but to his teachers, his friends, and most important, to that still small voice inside him.

Before I would be able to work with him on auditory skills, though, I also knew I was going to have to determine why he wasn't listening in the first place. When Brandan was a toddler I thought his aptitude for ignoring me was a result of his immaturity. When he was in kindergarten, I blamed it on bad parenting. During his early elementary years, I blamed it on the fact that he was a dreamer. As he grew older there were times when I was sure that Brandan could not concentrate on my words because he was too caught up in the moment to view the consequences. There were also times when I thought that maybe it was the opposite. Maybe Brandan was too much of a visionary to be bothered with such petty details.

Now I know that Brandan's inability to process and follow through on what I tell him is a combination of all of these things. The reason he doesn't always pay attention is because he is after all a child, and the majority of children tend to be distracted. It is also because I don't always use the most effective methods to get him to mind me. Furthermore, Brandan's selective hearing can also be attributed to the fact he is what many people would label as a daydreamer; his mind wanders quite a bit. Adding to the mix of all of these reasons is that he is just as likely to be hyperfocused on the task at hand. He gets so caught up in the moment that he literally blocks out everyone and everything.

Although these explanations sound quite contradictory, they are really complementary. All of these attributions are a result of Brandan's intense need to live every single moment to the fullest. Sometimes that moment is best lived by drowning out unwanted criticisms and demands. Sometimes that moment is best served by expanding and savoring it. Sometimes it is best served by simply disobeying authority. Other times it is a matter of him being too immature to follow through on what is being asked.

Once I realized Brandan wasn't complying not out of meanness but as a result of his intense personality, I began to look for ways to rectify the problem. Surely I could come up with a solution that would get him to focus in on, and pay attention to, what other people were saying. I soon found that the solutions, like the reasons behind the problem, were just as complex. Fine-tuning Brandan's listening skills was not going to be easy. Over the years, I have tried screaming, threatening, forcing, parroting, and pleading. Some of these methods have worked; most of them have not.

Screaming is of course the easiest, and to some parents the most logical approach, to getting a child to pay attention. It is easy because, with the exception of straining their voices, parents have to put very little physical exertion into it. Screaming also seems like the most logical approach because parents assume that the child is not hearing in the first place. But, again, hearing isn't the problem. Paying attention is. In the long run, screaming rarely works; mainly because children eventually become immune to it. Unless the directive is given in a particularly high-pitched or ear-shattering tone, they simply don't hear it. Children also tend to learn that screaming gets other people's attention, and they mimic this behavior to get what they want. Additionally, screaming is hard on everyone's nerves, and makes a statement that alerts everyone in the general vicinity that not only is the child out of control, but the parent is, too.

The same can be said of threatening. Threatening a highly active child rarely works unless the consequence is immediate. Spirited children who are caught up in an intense, thrill-of-the-moment activity want to expand the moment, not cut it short. Because they have a problem with delaying gratification, they will more often than not opt to continue expanding the moment rather than face a consequence that is hours away. The only time threatening does work is if the consequence is real and immediate. By being real, the consequence must mean something to them. The punishment must hit them where they hurt, so to speak. By being immediate, the consequence must happen right away. It cannot be something that will happen next week, tomorrow, or even later in the day. It has to be enforced at the exact moment of insubordination. If Brandan does not do a chore when I ask, then he has an additional chore added immediately. For example, if he does not take out the trash after being told to, then he not only has to take out the trash, but he has to put away the dishes.

Parroting, which I frequently refer to as my broken-record technique, is not the best alternative to threatening or screaming, but it does tend to work at times. The main reason it catches Brandan's attention is that it is extremely irritating. It keeps him from enjoying and expanding the moment he's caught up in. In other words, he complies just to stop the annoyance. Parroting a child's name over and over also makes the request sound urgent.

Using the broken-record technique does have its drawbacks, though. For one thing it can backfire. Brandan eventually reached a point where, whenever he wanted to get my attention, he would use this technique on me. Hearing the words "Mom, can I have that toy? Mom, can I have that toy?

Mom, can I have that toy?" over and over is enough to make a parent cave into anything. Another disadvantage to using this technique is that, like screaming, children eventually become immune to it, especially if it is used too often.

Pleading is probably the most useless of any of the tactics I have used. Besides being humiliating to the parent, it rarely works. Parents only use it on the assumption that their child can reason or will be willing to take pity on them. But highly active children, like all children, are usually too immature to willingly exchange their needs for someone else's.

I have found the best way to get Brandan to listen to me is a three-step approach. The first step involves making eye contact with him. Sometimes gaining eye contact can be as easy as simply stating his name. Other times it is not so easy. I have to physically touch him on the shoulder, or in extreme cases, take his face and direct it toward mine, in order to get him to look at me. Making eye contact is important because it takes the attention off of whatever Brandan is doing, and focuses it on me.

The second step involves stating what I want Brandan to do in a clear voice, using as few words as possible. I have found this to be critical. The fewer words I use, the more likely he is to pay attention. If I have to use more than seven or eight words, or more than two or three sentences, it begins to sound like I am giving a speech, and nothing turns Brandan off faster than a lecture on something he knows he doesn't want to do in the first place.

The third step involves using a set time for when the action needs to take place. If the action needs to be followed through on immediately, such as in the case of Brandan putting on his coat, I always use the word "now." Although "now" is usually implied, for some reason Brandan does not always understand that. I have found that most highly active children simply don't understand inferences. Therefore, it is best for parents and caregivers to be as clear as possible as to when they expect the action to take place.

In addition to using this three-step approach, I have also found that using gestures helps Brandan to pay attention to what I am saying. For example, if I want him to take out the trash, I make eye contact by simultaneously saying his name and touching him on the shoulder. Once I have his attention, I state my directive, "Take the trash out now," while using a gesture that simulates the act of lifting.

If Brandan does not comply after the first request, I know that it is imperative that I follow through by physically making him do it. Even if it embarrasses the both of us. After a few times of physically removing Brandan from a situation, he has become much more compliant. In fact, it has now reached a point where Brandan complies almost immediately, especially in public, because he wants to avoid the humiliation of a showdown with me.

In hindsight, I see that I could have saved a lot of time and anguish on that snowy New Year's Day if I had simply jerked Brandan back in the house after my first request to put on a coat. But freeing a highly active child's spirit is not an easy thing. It is a learn as you go curriculum. I am certain that over the years I will need to come up with additional approaches to getting and keeping Brandan's attention. I'm sure it will be just another of one of the many ongoing challenges in which I will have to think up new and creative ways to let his spirit soar. I also know, though, that like all the other steps I have taken to ensure my son's emancipation, my efforts to harmonize his energy with the outside world will be rewarded in the long run.

14

Fostering Friendships

The doorbell rings for the fourth time in five minutes. My eleven-year-old gatekeeper/birthday boy promptly answers it, and another one of his friends blasts through the entrance, his sleeping bag under one arm, his overnight bag in the other.

Brandan and his comrade disappear up the stairs before I have reached the foyer. I notice the guest's father standing on the porch and invite him in. He smiles and wisely declines the offer. I shut the door and return to the kitchen to put the finishing touches on Brandan's birthday cake. Only half of the expected guests have arrived and already the house sounds as if a prison break is under way.

The doorbell rings again. This time, the pandemonium upstairs has distracted Brandan long enough for me to answer it first. It is another father, with twins in tow. Thankfully, these boys don't look anything alike and I don't have to worry about confusing their names. The pair follow the sound of the uproar as the father mumbles "good luck" before retreating to his SUV.

Just as I am about to close the door, another car pulls up. The boy's mother, who also happens to be a friend of mine, accompanies her son to the front door. I ask her if she wants to stay, but she shakes her head no. She and her husband are going to the movies. The roar from Brandan's room intensifies, and the newly arrived guest doesn't bother with manners. He snatches his bag from his mother's arms and races up the stairs. His mother covers her ears and asks if I want to come with her. I am tempted to say yes, but know that there is no way that my husband will be able to handle the party alone. I reluctantly bid adieu and head in the direction of the chaos.

I dodge through the trail of scattered sleeping bags, pillows, and overnight backpacks that line the hallway to Brandan's room. Throwing open the bedroom door, I see the three-ring circus is definitely under way. Two guests are jumping on the bed. Two others are on the floor wrestling. One boy is rummaging through the closet, pulling out every available toy. Another is on the Internet, conversing in an adult chat room. The birthday boy is nowhere to be seen.

"Where's Brandan?" I ask.

No one responds.

"Get off the bed," I yell to the two boys who are using the mattress as a trampoline. They immediately oblige. I turn off the computer and ask again, "Where's Brandan?" The disappointed, web-savvy guest answers that he is getting some snacks from the kitchen. I go down the stairs and sure enough Brandan has retrieved every available junk food item from the pantry.

"Don't take that stuff upstairs," I tell Brandan. "I'm ordering pizza."

"What kind?" he asks.

"What kind do you want?"

"Let me see," he says, galloping up the stairs. I quickly follow. Partly because I want to help him get the order. Partly because I want to make sure that the two gymnasts aren't still jumping on the mattress.

Thankfully, the bed is empty. However, all the boys are swarming like flies on honey around the computer. I nudge my way through the troops to see what's up. Apparently, they have logged back onto the Internet in record time and are "innocently" chatting with a teenage girl. By the writing skills of this online buddy, I can see that she is anything but innocent. It seems as though the boys have also lead her to believe that they are not so chaste, either. Much to everyone's dismay, I immediately terminate the conversation by typing "find someone your own age." I then pull the plug on the Internet iniquity by confiscating the telephone cable.

In an effort to redirect the boys, I offer up pizza.

"Pepperoni, cheese, meatball, sausage, no sausages, extra olives, no olives, extra cheese." The commands continue until I announce that I will be ordering four large pizzas; two with extra cheese, one with pepperoni, and one with half sausage, half olives. The proclamation temporarily silences the mob, and I go downstairs to finish putting out the plates and other party utensils.

Five minutes later Brandan is back in the kitchen. "There is nothing to do," he complains. With seven boys in the house, I find this hard to believe, but suggest that we rent some movies. Brandan agrees and gathers up his accomplices. I give my husband the pizza order and load the boys into the minivan.

Brandan is the first to retrieve his selections at the store. However, he has somehow gotten the notion that now that he is eleven he will be able to rent M-rated games and R-rated movies. I immediately tell him to return the inappropriate material and choose something suitable for eleven-year-old boys. Meanwhile, his friends seem to have the same idea and produce equally distasteful selections. Amazed at their tenacity, I shake my head no.

Finally, after thirty minutes of pawing over every single video game and movie in the store, Brandan and his guests make some appropriate choices and we are back in the van, headed for home.

By the time we get back to the house, two additional guests have arrived and another is on the phone requesting a ride to the party. It seems his mother is working late, and he has no way of getting to our house. My pity level is incredibly low these days, and I reluctantly agree to pick him up. Brandan is overjoyed, as this boy, who is also highly active, is always the life of every party. The ride to retrieve the child is relatively short, and by the time we get back home, the pizzas have arrived. The boys descend on the food like wolves after a fallen deer.

After dinner, Brandan and his ten guests take the two video games and three movies up to his room. My husband comments that overnight parties aren't so bad. I remind him that we still have twelve hours to go. Besides that, I have yet to get through a child's birthday party, especially one that requires sleep deprivation, where tears weren't involved. My prediction is correct, when, thirty minutes later, Brandan is downstairs crying.

"No one is listening to me. They won't watch what I want to watch and they're tearing up my room," he moans.

I lead him back up the stairs to investigate. Sure enough, the room is demolished. The sheets and comforter have been stripped from the bed, the bookshelves and closets have been emptied, and there is not an inch of floor space to walk on.

I immediately assign cleanup tasks to all the boys, including Brandan. Within minutes the room is back in order. But Brandan's feelings are not so easily repaired. I suggest that we eat the cake and open the presents. This proposal sends the boys stampeding down the stairs. By the time I arrive, most of the presents have been unwrapped. I stop Brandan from opening any more until we have eaten the birthday cake.

My husband corrals the herd into the kitchen while I light eleven miniature sparklers. The fizzing candles spew sparks of fire all over the table, and the boys become momentarily mesmerized long enough to sing a short and offbeat rendition of "Happy Birthday." While the cake and ice cream are being consumed, I am given a chance to rest. My repose is interrupted by the crackling sound of wrapping paper. I force myself off the couch and back to the living room to find Brandan and his friends pawing the paper off the last few gifts. Once again I stop Brandan and make him pick up the trash. After the gifts have been organized and recorded on his list for thank-you notes, I direct the boys upstairs to watch a video.

I should have known to be more specific. Two minutes later Brandan is back downstairs with one of his friends, complaining about another one of the guest's inability to "follow directions."

"Whose directions is he not following?" my husband asks.

"Mine," is Brandan's obvious answer.

My husband tells him that he needs to get along with all of his guests. However, Brandan's eyes begin to tear up. "This isn't how my party is supposed to go. Everyone is doing anything they want to do, and no one is doing what I tell them to do."

I remind Brandan that when you have this many guests, things are going to get out of control. This explanation is as much for my sake as it is for his. I should have known to limit the party to three or four boys. Fortunately and unfortunately, though, Brandan makes friends very easily, and he truly does have an abundance of close companions.

I decide the best thing to do at the moment is to mobilize the troops and go for a walk. One boy suggests that I allow them to play "ding dong ditch." I fondly remember my own days of causing mischief in the neighborhood with my two brothers, but then remember that I am now a responsible adult. I try to act shocked as I decline. A resounding boo reverberates through the crowd.

"However, we can take the dog and go down to the school playground." My suggestion is met with a round of hurrahs. Nothing is more exciting than being at the park at night when no one else is around.

After putting my German shepherd, Tina, on a leash, the boys and I make our way two blocks to the school. It is 10 P.M. and pitch black outside, and I am glad that we have the dog with us. Though I can't imagine who would want to mug a gang of wild, eleven-year-old boys, one can't be too careful.

Brandan and his friends are thrilled to be loose at this hour of the night, and jog ahead. By the time I arrive at the playground, the boys are hanging upside down from the equipment. I find a bench and take a seat with my dog, Tina, next to me.

Suddenly, a man and his dog appear out of the dark. Tina and I are both startled. One of the boys on the equipment is as well, and he screams. Tina interprets a threat in the situation and jerks on her leash. I pull back, but the man continues walking toward us. Before I know it, Tina has slipped out of her collar and is charging the man's dog. I am horrified and chase after her. I get between her and the stranger, but spend the next five minutes trying to get Tina back in her collar. She won't obey. Not only do my children seem to have selective hearing, but my dog does, too. The man begins to swear at Tina. He threatens to call the police if I don't get her and the boys under control. I am humiliated. Not only do I seemingly have no control over my children, I have no control over my dog.

Finally, one of the eleven-year-old guests tackles the ninety-pound canine, and she is back on the leash. I vow never to take this many boys, or my dog, down to the park again. As we head back home, Brandan is overcome with grief. He is sure that the authorities will come and take Tina away.

I tell Brandan that the man was mad, but that he won't be calling anyone. Brandan is still upset. His friends console him. One of the boys puts his arm around Brandan's shoulder; several others pat him on the back. They talk about the man at the playground, trading stories about him as we make our way home through the dark streets. They are sure this stranger was out to attack us, and that is why Tina was chasing him. They talk about what a good dog Tina is and how she would not let the man hurt us.

I feel a warmth for Brandan's friends as I listen to them recount the story over and over. Although I know that this poor man was simply out for a walk with his dog, I understand that, in their own way, the boys are trying to take a bad situation and make it better.

With every few steps the tales are embellished. One boy confesses that the stranger tried to kick him. Another swears that he hit him in the head. One boy pipes up that he knows the man, and that he hates children and dogs. By the time we arrived on the doorstep, legend has it that this man stalks children at night in the park. Although I am aghast at how quickly the recanting of an event can get out of hand, I can see that the exaggeration is making Brandan feel much better.

The remainder of the soiree is fraught with sleepless boys, spilled drinks, and various other skirmishes. In general, though, there is a camaraderie about the event at the playground. These ten eleven-year-old boys share a story and a battle, and they dine on the account into the wee hours. Even as their parents arrive in the morning, the story is as fresh as if it happened minutes earlier. The enemy has become the connection, the rallying cry, the bonding event that binds them as one.

HAVING SURVIVED MY son's birthday party and witnessed the aftereffects of September 11, I am reminded that although friendships may be ignited by common ideals, they are solidified by traumatic experiences. This is especially true when the event is highlighted by a sudden awareness of our own vulnerability. Whether we are citizens of a country, or eleven-year-old boys out on a walk with friends, experiencing an assault, real or perceived, is enough to reinforce our belief that strength lies in numbers.

This reliance on numbers makes us circle our wagons. It is what makes us phone everyone we know when a catastrophe happens, even if the disaster is on the other side of the country. Love may make the world go round, but security is the glue that binds us to one another whether we are eight or eighty. It is truly the foundation upon which most of our friendships are based.

This connection is never more evident then in highly active children. Highly active children, especially boys, love to run in packs. Being a part of a group guarantees camaraderie for these children, but it also insures instant protection from outsiders. In a way, childhood, as well adult friendships, form an invisible shield against those who would cause emotional, spiritual, or physical harm. They also bring a sense of acceptance and belonging to children who are already questioning their place in the world.

Over the years I have marveled at my son's ability to seek out and make friends. To Brandan, nothing is worth doing if it's not done with someone else. He first learned to introduce himself at two, and was fraternizing with the other boys at the McDonald's ball bin by the time he was three. Since then, he has been seeking out and making friends as though he were running for political office. One might even say that he craves companionship—lots of it.

At first his perpetual desire to have a lot of buddies bothered me. I worried that he was too needy, that he depended too much on others, and that he should learn to feel comfortable being alone. Eventually I came to understand that while some of his need for companionship may arise from being bored or lonely, most of it stems from his belief that strength lies in numbers. It is his way of protecting himself from unknown assaults in an unpredictable world. While his friendships may appear to be started by a shared interest in football or girls, they are bound by his need to fortify himself.

For the most part, this compulsion to have plenty of pals can be positive. It requires Brandan to stay on top of his social skills, gives him someone with whom to share his innermost feelings and thoughts, and frees up time for me. But like most blessings, having an extremely sociable child is a double-edged sword. The need to have lots of friends also makes Brandan, and other highly active children, susceptible to peer pressure.

When Brandan is running with a pack of friends, rather than just one or two individuals, he is more easily coerced into engaging in activities he wouldn't ordinarily undertake. While there may be safety in numbers, it is also the very numbers themselves that can cause a problem. This feeling of safety can quickly turn into a feeling of bravery as highly active children continue to push the already-over-the-edge envelope.

I have no doubt that if I hadn't supervised the boys outside that night at Brandan's party that they would have gotten into some sort of mischief. While it may have been something as harmless as ringing a neighbor's doorbell and running away, or something more dangerous such as throwing rocks at cars, it would have most assuredly been something that they would not have even considered doing alone.

Furthermore, in addition to pumping up the confidence and courage to engage in mischief, the larger the group, the more pressure each child is under to be the ringleader. In fact, a leisurely evening with friends can quickly turn into a competition to see who can cause the most trouble. Leaders have to think of unique ways to keep the troops amused, and when you are eleven, entertainment frequently takes the form of pranks.

Brandan has one particular friend who is the perfect example. This boy is nothing short of being a delinquent, and he is always thinking of unique and unusual ways to get himself, and those around him, into trouble. Yet all the boys love him. He is the perfect answer to adolescent angst. I have tried to discourage Brandan from playing with this boy, but he is like a magnet for my son, as well as every other child in the neighborhood, not only because he is entertaining, but because he is always on the cutting edge. He can be depended on to bring life to every party. I have finally resigned myself to the fact that this child is going to be an influence in my son's life whether I like it or not. Rather than trying to separate Brandan from this friend, I make a conscious effort to supervise both of the boys whenever they are together.

Although many highly active children are like Brandan and have an array of cohorts, there are also a significant number who are unable to make friends at all. This is especially true in the younger years, when a highly active child's wild behavior more directly affects his or her peers. During preschool and kindergarten, when they are less able to control their movements, their need to physically interact with other children becomes bothersome. Highly active children tend to have a hard time keeping their hands to themselves and are often seen as intrusive. This problem decreases as they grow older, but unfortunately by the time many highly active children begin to settle down, they have been permanently ostracized by the neighborhood or school kids. Once a child has been excluded by his peers, the only way to cultivate a social life for him or her is to change schools and start fresh.

I have found that highly active girls tend to be excluded for their conduct more frequently than highly active boys. I believe this is because wild behavior is generally more accepted in boys than in girls. Girls are expected by society to be in control of their activity level. When a spirited boy runs amok, parents, as well as teachers, turn their heads. When a spirited girl gets into trouble, she is immediately seen as a problem child, not only by adults, but also by her peers. She is therefore more likely to be banned from birthday parties and other social events. Girls seem unwilling to put up with misbehavior from their friends, while boys see this same misbehavior as positive.

In addition to being ostracized for their wild demeanor, highly active girls, as well as highly active boys, are frequently left out of the loop because they don't understand social cues. They always seem to be in fast-forward and frequently fail to read body language or other subtle nuances. This makes them seem indifferent or self-centered, which is truly sad because highly active children are extremely sensitive individuals.

Fortunately, there are many psychologists and therapists who specialize in teaching social skills, and group classes are said to be very helpful in assisting any child who can't seem to make friends. Some public school districts offer these classes, others may be found by checking your city's mental health center. Social skills classes usually meet once or twice a week, and a group of children are supervised by two or more therapists. Although social skills classes are available for all ages, I believe that they are most helpful for elementary school–aged children. A certain amount of maturity needs to be present before a highly active child will be able to pick up on the skills, and children under the age of six rarely have this. And although older adolescents would benefit from such a class, a parent would have to literally shanghai a teenager to get them to attend it. Most teenagers would rather die than acknowledge that they lack social skills.

Despite the success rate that psychologists claim for these classes, though, I feel that social skills are best modeled on a twenty-four/seven basis by a child's family. I don't believe intimacy and genuine trust can be learned in a clinical setting regardless of how proficient the moderator. Truly, it must be replicated on a continuous basis by loving parents in order for a child to learn to connect with another human being.

Sometimes, though, despite what a parent does to encourage social development, a child will still have a hard time fitting in at school, and won't be able to make friends. Eventually, he becomes the proverbial square peg in the round hole, which makes him easy prey for playground bullies.

Although one of the cardinal rules of traditional parenting is to stay out of a child's social life, I believe that there are certain times when direct interference by adults is necessary. Emotional abuse by peers can be just as dangerous to the child's well-being as physical abuse. Because a child who is being bullied is usually self-conscious about what is happening, this anger is then turned inward and he often becomes depressed and withdrawn. The anger can also be turned outward in fits of rage and revenge. Both responses are equally dangerous. In fact, it is this sort of continuous bullying and social intimidation that leads many children to retaliate through school shootings.

Thankfully, school administrators and teachers are getting the message that playground victims have been screaming for years, and stringent methods are finally being used to deal with bullies. However, I believe that parents still need to be vigilant in making sure that their child's school is a safe place, emotionally, physically, and spiritually. Freeing a child's spirit means more than just snipping off the labels and untying ropes. It also means protecting every child's basic, inalienable rights. Never is one of those rights, the pursuit of happiness, more consequential than when you are a highly active child in need of a friend.

15

What's Around the Bend: Redefining Success

"Wake up!"

The verbal assault forces me upright in bed. It is eight-thirty on a rainy Saturday morning. Brandan's head is hovering just inches from mine. His overnight guest is standing at my bedroom door.

"What do you want for breakfast?"

"Nothing," I mumble.

"Mom!"

I roll over and put the pillow over my head. My husband burrows under the sheets.

Brandan continues his badgering, finally pulling out the vocation card as a last resort. "How can I be a famous chef one day if I can't even cook breakfast?"

I peer at my son from under the pillow. His freckled face is beaming with confidence. "What happened to being a professional wrestler?" I mumble.

"Can't I be both?"

I can't help but smile. Most assuredly if there is ever going to be a master chef who is also a professional wrestler, it will be him. Guilt and the fact that I want to get more sleep get the better of me and I agree to let my rugged wrestler turned culinary craftsman cook breakfast. Brandan and his guest immediately retreat to the kitchen and begin rummaging through the refrigerator and pantry in search of food.

Minutes later my appetizer of one miniature muffin arrives along with a glass of orange juice. I obligingly plop the pastry in my mouth and lie back down.

"Where's the cooking spray?" Brandan asks. Resisting the temptation to inquire why, I don my robe and lead the boys into the kitchen. I put the spray next to the various-sized skillets that line the counter and try not to think about the impending mess as I head back to my room.

Predicting that I will once more be called to duty, I climb into bed with my robe on.

Seconds later, the doorbell rings. Two more of Brandan's friends join the impromptu cooking fest. It's amazing how I practically have to pry my son out of bed during the weekday, but on the weekend, he and his friends are up and about before the crack of dawn.

"Does your mom know you are making her breakfast?" I hear the most rational of his buddies ask.

I can't make out Brandan's reply, but it is met with laughter from the group.

After another few minutes of clattering from the kitchen, one of the boys appears at my bedside. "Brandan wants to know where the pepper is."

"I don't like pepper on my eggs," I fib.

The boy seems disappointed, but relays the message to Brandan.

Two seconds later this same boy is back. "Where is the egg beater?"

"Use a fork," I reply.

The clanging of pots and pans keeps me from closing my eyes. Thinking about a similar episode on the *I Love Lucy* show, I speculate about how much longer I should let this charade go on before agreeing to cook my own breakfast. Just as I am about ready to climb out of my cozy nest to investigate, my second course, a large platter of scrambled eggs, arrives. From the look of the fluffy yellow heap, the boys must have used the entire carton.

I sit up in bed and take a bite. Shifting back and forth from foot to foot, the budding chefs anxiously await my approval. The eggs are somewhat undercooked, but not bad. I nod at the boys and consume several more forkfuls before placing the plate on the nightstand.

"Aren't you hungry?" Brandan asks.

I affirm that I am, but that I need to rest.

"Would you like some, too, Dad?"

My wise husband feigns sleep.

The boys retreat to their post in the kitchen to decide on the main course. Meanwhile I try to remember how blessed I am to have a son who is willing to cook for me. Brandan has matured so quickly these past three years. Before I know it, he will be out of the house and there will be no more rude awakenings, no more early-morning doorbell ringings by friends, no more dirty kitchens to clean up. I am saddened by the thought. Having become accustomed to the constant turmoil and uproar that comes with having a highly active child, I know my life will feel like an empty tomb once Brandan and Amanda are grown.

A loud buzzing noise interrupts my poignant pondering. From the bedroom it sounds like the timer on the microwave. After minutes of unusual silence, I decide to investigate. As suspected, the mess hall is living up to its name. I navigate past a heap of dirty pans, cracked egg shells, spilled orange juice, and a crumbled bag of opened muffins over to the oven. An unknown slimy substance adhering to the bottom of my left foot makes a snapping noise with every move. Fearing the worst, I don't look down.

I reach around the empty package and open the microwave door. A heap of tangled black bacon marinating in two inches of grease is sizzling on a plate. I decide to leave it in the microwave and head back to my room.

Just as I am climbing into bed, I hear an "Oh no!" from upstairs, along with the clamoring of feet as the boys sprint down the steps and into the kitchen.

Moments later the master chef and his assistants appear at my door with their pièce de résistance. The boys watch with anticipation as I unravel a crunchy, black strip and slide it into my mouth. I nod my approval and graciously finish off my gift.

THREE YEARS HAVE passed since Brandan was taken off stimulants; three years since I regained my sanity and realized that what my son needed was latitude and love, not Ritalin and ropes. Brandan has made some incredible strides since I first made the decision to turn him loose on the world. He no longer needs help in falling asleep. He is more aware of his responsibilities in the family and at school, and he is more confident and self-assured then ever. In fact, now that he is eleven, Brandan is not all that different from his peers. Of course, he is still more impulsive, more active, and more mischievous than the other boys his age, but he is also kinder and much more generous. I have also noticed that he laughs a lot more than any of his friends.

I worry as much about him as I ever did. However, my concerns have shifted. Instead of obsessing about disorders and remedies, I find myself obsessing about his future. I can't help but worry what new calamities the coming years will bring. Exactly how long will I be able to bump along behind his boat before some unforeseen turbulence bounces me on my backside?

I have tried to teach Brandan how to monitor himself, listen to others, make and keep friends, and direct his energy, but in my heart I know that he will continue to speed recklessly through life, sampling every dessert, cutting every corner, and chasing every star. In fact, I am sure that he will probably still be coloring outside of the lines whether he is eighteen or eighty. Like most teenagers he will also have his moments of anger and rebellion. There will be times when I won't be able to talk to him, much less connect with him in the meaningful way I have in the past.

In anticipating Brandan's future, though, I am at least comforted by the fact that there are many inspiring reports of celebrated adults who were considered highly active as children. Benjamin Franklin and Thomas Edison, not to mention a predominant number of presidents from George Washington to George W. Bush come to mind, as do artists such as Leonardo da Vinci and Michelangelo.

Although most of the famous people rumored to have attention deficit hyperactivity disorder were not officially diagnosed, I can't help but notice that they still share the same characteristics as Brandan. They are impulsive, highly active, inventive, and creative individuals. In fact, seeing Jim Carrey on a recent talk show made me think I was seeing a forty-year-old Brandan. And yet, Mr. Carrey, along with all the other famous people listed above, lack one thing that is quite common in highly active children today—the label of being disordered. Despite the pharmaceutical sand traps and educational mishaps, these celebrities and famous leaders have been able to sidestep the labels and go on to lead very successful lives. Not only have they been able to turn their disadvantages into advantages, they have literally parlayed them into fame and fortune.

Of course, there will be some clinicians who will say that for every Robin Williams or Jim Carrey there are thousands of ADHD adults who are incapable of functioning normally in society. They will argue that the Michelangelos and Ben Franklins of the world are flukes, not the norm. They may even compound the negative by pointing out that the majority of the prison population is considered ADHD. But I don't believe that these remarkable entertainers and world leaders have to be the exception any more than I think that highly active children are destined to be criminals.

Somewhere along the way these spirited individuals like Thomas Edison and Michelangelo were able to get a sense of their own divine nature. It was their ability to see themselves as unique and gifted, despite what the bystanders may have been telling them, that inspired them to make such wonderful contributions to the world. In essence, they made their mark on society because of their differences, not in spite of them.

I truly believe that if we can endow this same type of self-awareness and self-esteem in all our highly active children, then being the next Madonna or Jim Carrey truly would be the norm, rather than the exception. If we can free our children early enough and often enough, and empower them with our approval instead of our censure, then their success rates would drastically improve. Not only would our world be filled with creative, talented inventors and entertainers, but I'm betting that our prison population would drop 50 percent. On top of all that, I wouldn't be surprised if one of these active, generous, gifted, and liberated children came up with a peaceful solution to the problem in the Middle East.

This doesn't of course imply that freeing our highly active children's spirits will guarantee them a star on the Hollywood Walk of Fame or a Nobel Peace Prize, nor does it suggest that they will even be well-known in their fields. What it does mean is that every highly active child can be expected to make a unique and meaningful contribution to the world. By freeing their spirits, these children will then have permission to use their highly active nature to the best of their ability without ropes and ridicule, while at the same time finding a trade that highlights their strengths and balances their weaknesses.

In order for our children's spirits to be truly free in choosing a vocation, though, we first need to rethink what it means to be accomplished. As a society we need to redefine what it means to have a successful career and a successful life. Truly, expertise shouldn't be determined by how many formal degrees one has, prestige shouldn't be decided by whether one wears a suit or a smock, and a champion shouldn't indicate who crossed the finish line first. In fact, being a winner shouldn't haven't anything to do with whether one completed the race or not. Success should be about living up to one's own potential. It should be about finding a purpose in life and following it through, no matter where it leads.

Redefining success should start in the home, but it also needs to be implemented in the classroom. Educators need to continue to expand the options that are available to children who learn differently. The goal of teachers and parents alike should be to ferret out and focus on a child's area of strength and help him or her build on it. True success is met only by doing what one does best, and for highly active children that can be a whole host of things.

In general, highly active children make great entrepreneurs. In fact, they are the ones that construct lemonade stands during the summer months and sell the most fundraising items at Christmastime. They are also incredibly creative individuals, and when given the freedom to experiment, they have the potential to be world-renowned inventors. In addition to being adept in sales and science, their natural characteristics, such as being the class clown, often lead them into the limelight where they make great entertainers.

I have tried in earnest to predict what Brandan will be when he grows up. However, like most children his age, his career choices change with every passing day. At this moment he wants to be a chef or a professional wrestler, but I know that by next month, or even next week, he will be chasing a different star. During his short lifetime he has counted computer programmer, construction worker, magician, football player, basketball player, baseball player, businessman, and golfer among his desired professions. He may grow up to be one of the above or something totally different. He may even be all of them at one time or another. Although he will never be an avid reader or have terrific handwriting, I have faith that he will be able to make a positive difference in the world in his own way.

I can only hope that the rewards that Brandan will reap by being true to his nature will far outweigh any obstacles he encounters along his path. I am also relying on the fact that my husband and I have at least forged a strong enough bond with our son that together we will be able to withstand any storms that lurk around the bend. In the long run, I believe it will be the millions of fleeting moments that we shared that will be the saving grace for Brandan. It will be an accumulation of the bedtime bonding, the gametime girding, and the suppertime slipknots. It will be every hug, every kiss, every word of encouragement that we offered our son that will keep him upright and on his feet in the midst of life's hurricanes.

When it comes down to it, though, the world is an uncertain place, and the truth is that I don't really know for sure what will become of Brandan, or of my daughter, Amanda, for that matter. Who can say what is around the bend for any of us? Nothing is absolute. Life is a crapshoot. The only guarantee is that there are no guarantees. Like all parents, those of us with highly active children will just have to keep our fingers crossed. We will have to continue to hang on tight as best we can, taking every day as it comes, and praying that the bumps are few and far between.

And so, as our family begins to whiz its way around the jagged cliffs of adolescence, I brace myself for the uncertainties that lie just beyond the bend, armed only with one conviction—that the ability to live fully in the present, smelling every rose, tasting every treat, and viewing every landscape is truly one of God's greatest gifts of all. My highly active, courageously spirited, incredibly talented son taught me that lesson. And, no matter what the future holds for him, I wouldn't trade my frenzied trip on the seat of his pants for all the assurances in the world.

Resources

WEBSITES

ADHD.kids.tripod.com (Outside the Box)

ADDResource.com

PSparents.net

focusonadd.com

RECOMMENDED READING

Ritalin Is Not the Answer, by Dr. David Stein

The Wonder of Boys and *A Fine Young Man,* by Michael Gurian

The Myth of the A.D.D. Child, by Thomas Armstrong

Attention Deficit Disorder: A Different Perception and *ADD Success Stories,* by Thom Hartmann